Waking Up in the Men's Room

Waking Up

in the Men's Room

a memoir

Catherine Macleod

BETWEEN THE LINES

TORONTO

Waking Up in the Men's Room: A Memoir
© Catherine Macleod, 1998

Between the Lines gratefully acknowledges financial assistance for our publishing activities from the Ontario Arts Council, The Canada Council for the Arts, and the Government of Canada through the Book Publishing Industry Development Program.

Every reasonable effort has been made to find copyright holders. The publisher would be pleased to have any errors or omissions brought to its attention.

Canadian Cataloguing in Publication Data
Macleod, Catherine, 1948-
      Waking up in the men's room : a memoir
ISBN 1-896357-07-5
1. Macleod, Catherine, 1948– . 2. Feminism – Canada. 3. Trade-unions and the arts – Canada. 4. Social movements – Canada. 5. Feminists – Canada – Biography. 6. Trade-unions – Canada – Officials and employees – Biography. I. Title.
HQ1455.M324A3 1998   305.42'092   C98-930684-4

Cover and text design: Counterpunch / Linda Gustafson
Printed in Canada by Transcontinental

1 2 3 4 5 6 7 8 9 10   05 04 03 02 01 00 99 98

Between the Lines
720 Bathurst Street, #404, Toronto, Ontario, M5S 2R4, Canada
(416) 535-9914   www.btl.on.ca

Dedication

For my mother

Catherine Corr Kiltie Macleod

(1917-1986)

Contents

Acknowledgements

*It takes a whole village to raise a child. It also takes a whole
village to create a book. I would like to thank the villagers
who helped raise this work:*

*the family who lived with it — my father Bob Macleod,
my husband Martin Quinn, our children Grayson, Joseph,
and Katheryne;*

*the considerate friends who read drafts and in so doing
helped it grow along the way — Maja Ardal, Karl Beveridge,
Carole Condé, Julie Davis, Vincenzo Pietropaolo, Sid Ryan,
Adrianna Tetley, and Laura Weintraub;*

the other friends at Between the Lines, Our Times *and
Flat Singles Press who always encouraged me to express not
just what I thought but also what I felt — Lorraine Endicott,
Paul Eprile, Phil Hall, Marg Anne Morrison, and Jamie Swift;*

*my brave editor Robert Clarke who made the ground it
covers as solid as possible;*

*the Ontario Arts Council and the Canada Council for
funding support;*

*and finally, all my brothers and sisters in the social justice
movement who made room for the writer at their tables. In
particular I thank Ron Dickson, D'Arcy Martin, and
Mercedes Steedman.*

Prologue

In the Alcoholics Anonymous tradition, it is customary for a speaker to begin a talk with some qualifying statements; to outline briefly why they believe they have the right to speak. It is as good a way to begin a story as any.

I might start by saying that when I was a child, and under the daily authority and tremendous influence of my Catholic teachers, I had decided that I had a religious vocation and that my life could have meaning if I became a nun and helped people. Nuns seemed to be women of the world, unencumbered by the rigours of the domestic lives that drew the colour from the faces of my mother and my aunts. I might say that, like an earlier notion I had about becoming an artist, my new obsession elicited my father's stern disapproval. And at that age, little did I know of the problems I might have with taking strict vows of poverty, obedience, and chastity.

Maybe it would be best to start by showing the group a photograph of my son Grayson – the one that shows his tattoos, the one I took of him the day he came home at age eighteen, after being away for so long. Or a picture of young Katheryne Schulz, who became a daughter to me at age fifteen, shortly after her mother and my closest friend Pat died. And the picture of Martin, my husband, and his son Joseph, standing outside the greenhouses in Strathroy, Ontario. Maybe it would be best to start with my family. After all, the fight for my right to belong to a family, to love and to be loved, in an age that had reshaped and restructured the family beyond recognition, has been a central preoccupation of mine.

Perhaps I shouldn't mention that I call myself a poet, a feminist, an anti-racist, or a socialist, because those road signs I tend to use lead in so many directions. They invite too many questions. Labels are seldom adequate to their hulking tasks. It might be enough to turn to what Northrop Frye calls "The Great Code" and read aloud the piece of scripture I have in my notebook. I found it while reading about the history of the Co-operative Commonwealth Federation and the New Democratic Party, in a story about the arrests that took place during the Winnipeg General Strike in 1919, when the famous socialist leader J.S. Woodsworth was taken into custody and charged with "uttering seditious words." Woodsworth had been defending the rights of the working class, and his alleged crime included publishing words from Isaiah: "And they shall build houses, and inhabit them; and they shall plant vineyards, and eat the fruit of them. They shall not build, and another inhabit; they shall not plant, and another eat; for as the days of a tree are the days of my people, and mine elect shall long enjoy the work of their hands."

I would have to say, though, that many of my ideas about love and justice are based on values driven into me by my mother and my early Catholic teachers, most of them women. And as much as I have tried to distance myself from them, it was from them I learned the basic lessons about right and wrong. Joan Baez and Bob Dylan may have set my golden rules to music in the 1960s, but the Corporal Works of Mercy alone were enough to turn me into a socialist: feed the hungry, give drink to the thirsty, clothe the naked, shelter the homeless, visit the sick, ransom the captive, and bury the dead. Perhaps surprisingly, it was during my work and life in the labour movement, learning from working-class people, that I was most able to practise these principles.

I might mention a book of essays I had been reading on St. John of the Cross, the sixteenth-century Carmelite mystic. Like his mentor, Teresa of Avila, John was convinced that suffering – that thing we fight to the death to avoid – was the key to understanding and enlightenment. As a young girl I used to shout in misery and annoyance when my mother pulled her stiff brush through the wet tangles of my long hair. "You have to suffer to be beautiful," she said to me more than once. A domestic ritual of power, pain, and resistance characterized my relationship with my mother for most of my life.

By the time I graduated from Our Lady of Sorrows Separate School I was well-versed in the lives of the saints and the role of martyrdom – the last shall be first, the meek shall inherit the earth, and all that. It is okay to be meek. It is okay to be last. The teachings emphasized suffering for the sake of suffering – masochism. They ignored the empowering spiritual imperative – resistance – equally explicit in the stories of the martyrs, from Katherine of Alexandria on her wheel of nails to St. Daniel in the den of lions.

I cannot dispute that suffering is *one* fact of life, but I'm no fan of the concept. I would do almost anything to avoid suffering, and have; but when I have had no option, I have slowly learned to face it. Sometimes I have examined suffering with the help of psychoanalysis, sometimes I have read books about how others have coped with similar situations, sometimes I have talked about it with friends, and sometimes I have just sat it out, like someone watching a violent thunderstorm, until it passes. But I only found something like a sense of emancipation when I finally coupled the passive word "suffering" with its active partner "struggle."

In the end, all of this might lead me to find something new – a resolve, a plan of action, a name for something that was nameless, an understanding. Without an active engagement these insights might have eluded me; and what is worse, they might have prevented me from appreciating that other, if opposite, durable fact of life – joy.

I learned on my own particular trip through the cultural revolution that there was much unacknowledged and private suffering, and many contradictions, in all political and social systems – left and right, patriarchal and feminist. I also learned that my natural rebelliousness, my genuine resistance to suffering, and my sometimes raging desire for change, could be exploited. Perhaps I was "easily led," and others could take advantage of my youthful faith in their leadership. While they helped me to reject some big ideas – the supremacy of the white race, the sacredness of wealth, and the inferiority of women – too often I let well-meaning others prescribe the forms that my rebellions would take. I was often unable to articulate, in ways true to my own experience, the meaning of my own life and values.

While the good people in Alcoholics Anonymous use the "qualifying" method in their practice, teachers such as bell hooks and students of Paulo Freire employ the "confessional narrative" in what they call their "decolonizing political and spiritual practice." This book is my attempt to "qualify." It is my confessional narrative, my attempt to make sense of my years so far, to recapture some of the times – good and bad – and remember some of the people who travelled with me.

I have been helped in this by a small book that I have read and reread during the past few years, Rainer Maria Rilke's *Letters to a Young Poet*, a modern translation of letters sent to a young military student at the turn of the century. Trust yourself, the book said to me. If it turns out you are wrong, the natural growth of your inner life will eventually guide you to other insights. "Allow your judgements their own silent, undisturbed development, which, like all progress, must come from deep within and cannot be forced or hastened."

But I must caution you about the story I am about to tell – warn you that it is just one version of a story that involved many others, and each of those others has their own story to tell about the same times and places. More than that, it is only one version of a story that I myself could tell you in a hundred different ways. I have forgotten much and remembered imperfectly much more. My imagination has carried and refined some of these stories for so long that I even wonder if they belong to me at all. All I can ask is that you allow me, as I invite you by this telling, to create at least one plausible meaning from a shared experience, that for the most part is still completely unaccounted for.

Catherine Macleod
Kincardine, Ontario
April 1998

Waking Up in the Men's Room

We cannot think of our biographies only as time-bound, a progression along a line from birth to death. This is only one dimension, the temporal one, a linear one.

The soul moves in circles, said Plotinus. Hence our lives are not moving straight ahead; instead, hovering, wavering, returning, renewing, repeating. The genes work in lags and spurts. The sense of being "in the zone," in touch, opened out, blasted, seeing and knowing, comes and goes utterly unpredictably, yet with stable patterns.

I am different from everyone else and the same as everyone else; I am different from myself ten years ago and the same as myself ten years ago; my life is a stable chaos, chaotic and repetitive both, and I can never predict what tiny, trivial bit of input will result in a huge and significant output. I must always remain acutely sensitive to initial conditions, such as what or who came into the world with me and enters the world with me each day. On that I remain dependent.

James Hillman, *The Soul's Code:*
In Search of Character and Calling (1996)

Industry's Orphans

RECENTLY, AFTER READING *Growing up in the Gorbals*, an account by psychologist and economist Ralph Glasser of the 1920s and 1930s in a Glasgow working-class district, I dug out a photograph of my family taken in late 1949. At the time, our family was living in Govan, an area that stood cheek to cheek with the Gorbals. In the photo my father has my baby brother Robert on his knee. I am sitting on my mother's knee – a girl of one and a half staring directly into the lens with a look of pure terror.

Before cameras were affordable, a paid photographer would come to do annual family portraits in the grimy tenements where we lived. The appearance of this stranger in our house was a luxury and a ritual, and everyone got polished and shined for the record. The photo is black and white, but I remember the burgundy swirls of my mother's "best" dress, and I know my father's "good" shoes were brown suede. In my hair, which my mother had tugged and pulled into Shirley Temple ringlets for the occasion, is a big bow ribbon, which I know was a violet satin. You can see that my mother and father are a handsome couple. They could be famous actors playing the part of poor people in a kitchen-sink drama. They radiate a rebellious and shy confidence, in spite of the faded wallpaper and chipped baseboard behind them and the torn linoleum at their feet.

The Second World War was over, but it seemed like peace still had not arrived in our corner of the world. The war and the nightly bombings had been bad enough, but afterwards Glasgow, like much of Europe, was in ruins. I was not so young that I can't remember the bombed shipyards, the crumbling tenements with the ghosts of former rooms delineated only by their ridiculously different and cheerful flowered wallpapers. I remember fireplaces, still in the walls, suspended absurdly, one, two, and three storeys above a street. The families that had once warmed their hands and faces around them were long gone – dispersed, broken, relocated, dead. In Glasgow the collapse of the shipbuilding industry had begun, and my parents' universe was in tatters. Destruction, desolation, despair, drink, and delinquency were rampant. Everybody owed somebody money they couldn't pay. Those fast on their feet were running for cover, applying for immigration papers to the United States or Canada (which were thought to be the same) or to Australia or New Zealand. My parents were not the only ones trying to smile for the birdie and look their best for the future. There were thousands and thousands just like them. The shopkeepers, garment workers, skilled tradesmen, and labourers – Catholics, Protestants, and Jews alike – were packing themselves up and moving on.

In the postwar daze our neighbourhood, south of the River Clyde, was bulldozed off the map. It was the Glasgow city fathers themselves who had, in a colossal act of self-defeat, removed the Gorbals Cross. The square granite monument had stood in the heart of the working-class community for as far back as anyone could remember. My father told me that there had been an inscription on it, beneath the city's coat of arms, that you could read when you walked up a set of stone steps to the bronze fountain's basin. It read "Let Glasgow Flourish."

According to legend, Glasgow was founded in the sixth century A.D. by St. Kentigern, whose nickname is St. Mungo. His mother was St. Thenew, Scotland's first recorded rape victim, a battered woman and unwed mother. I encountered her legend in a little brochure I picked up on a visit to the People's Palace museum in Glasgow. The metaphorical power of Thenew's legend captivated me, reminding me of my own story, and the stories of so many other women, survivors in the man's world into which we were born female.

As the legend goes, Thenew disobeyed her father, a king, by refusing to marry the man he had chosen for her, and her father had her thrown out of the castle. The rejected suitor went after her and raped her, and when it became obvious that she was pregnant because of the rape, her father had her tossed from the top of a mountain. She miraculously survived, which made her father even more furious, and again he ordered her death. But the executioners, moved by compassion or conscience, couldn't carry out his command. They put her in a boat without oars or rudder and set her out to sea. Again, miraculously, Thenew survived. A shoal of fishes guided her boat to dry land at a place called Culross, where she gave birth to St. Mungo in A.D. 518. Her good son's memory is immortalized in a nursery rhyme that Glasgow children hear over and over again until it seems as though they were born with it on their lips. "*This is the bird that never flew/ this is the tree that never grew/ this is the bell that never rang/ this is the fish that never swam.*" The mother's story, though, seems to have no similarly popular song attached to it.

About a thousand years later a visitor described St. Mungo's city, Glasgow, as a large, fair, and well-built city, with pleasant broad streets. Another visitor noted its sweet air, delightful gardens, and orchards full of delicious fruits. When Daniel Defoe visited in 1725 he found it to be one of the cleanest, most beautiful, and finest-built cities in Great Britain.

By the 1820s the Industrial Revolution had changed all that. The hungry poured into the city from the Highlands, the neighbouring Lowlands, and Ireland to work in Glasgow's booming textile mills, shipyards, chemical factories, iron foundries, and manufacturing establishments. From December 1848 to March 1849, nearly fifty thousand Irish immigrants moved into the already overcrowded and bursting city heart. Not long after, a cholera epidemic crept through the filthy narrow back streets and into the cold, damp rooms in which the new industrial working class crowded. Since then my birth home has been called the armpit of the world.

Still, the working-poor Glaswegians had, through terrible hardship, created a tight and articulated political and social culture of their own.

These were a people who didn't expect to be millionaires. Hard work and pride in work were virtues and ends in themselves. Their material goals were moderate – comfort and job security – and a deep sense of fair play and justice seemed bred in their bones. They built a strong labour movement and fought for public education and health, among other things. The Scots were no fools. As early as 1865, with the Improvement Act, Scotland had already recognized that a free market and private philanthropy would never address the needs of the working poor.

This working class was Scotland's major postwar export, and its members, like my father, carried their values and culture with it. A lot of them would end up building the industrial boom in North America as highly respected skilled-trades workers. And many were responsible for the nature and gains of the industrial labour movement we know in Canada today. I have always carried their class, my class, like a locket in my fist.

The Second World War had turned Glasgow into a weary woman, too poor and tired to clean up the mess, her legendary strength drained, her legendary heart broken. My silent grandfather, Robert Corr, who had picked bodies out of smouldering buildings after the air raids, soon drank himself to death. My other grandfather, Robert Macleod, did the same. And the nightmare of Hitler was passed to me through the milk of my still shell-shocked mother. The recognition of post-traumatic stress syndrome and its treatment are recent knowledge. In my parents' time, those who survived the war had to muddle on the best they could, with their burdens of unspeakable, therefore unnamed, and best forgotten knowledge. I don't believe that such injuries ever really heal. Neglected, these injuries extend through time, carrying with them the appalling power to withhold a sense of personal peace forever. In the vulnerable and raw days that followed my mother's death in 1986, it hit me that I had never really understood her often repeated cry for "a minute's peace" – "Just one minute's peace. Is that too much to ask for?" she said more often than I like to remember.

My maternal grandmother, Margaret Corr, who worked as a seamstress in a garment factory, told me that Hitler created the grounds in which I had to play and grow. I learned to hate Hitler for his soup kitchens, his ration books, his alcoholism, his fights, his brutality on the streets, his unemployment, and all the other war wounds. She taught me to hate war.

My father took the official position. For him the war was over, and we had won. He worked six days a week and half of Sunday as a millwright in the shipyards and tried for a while to keep the news of the massive layoffs at a safe distance. Every Saturday night he would slip out of his greasy overalls and into better clothes and go out with the boys. I got to brush his brown suede shoes that seemed as long as my arms.

By the time the Battle of Britain was declared over, Glasgow's working class had been bombarded by not one but two aspiring world powers. Germany lost, but Hollywood didn't. American movies and stars, songs, fashions, and comic books had won the battle for hearts and minds. My father, seeing the magazine pictures of big cars and ranch-style bungalows, began to wonder if maybe the American way of life was just the answer to all the problems of the world he knew in Scotland. Like their Highland and Lowland and Irish ancestors who had emigrated before him, he could, I believe, see no other options.

Coming home drunk those Saturday nights he'd do his whisky millwright lament, to down the truth that nothing would ever be the way it used to be again. "Mona Lisa" was his song. "*Many dreams have been brought to your doorstep / but they just lie there / and they die there.*" He loved Nat King Cole. He'd belt that song out – right through the peeling wallpaper of that weary one-room tenement flat, called a "single end," right over our blitzed gardens, and send it tumbling onto the rubble streets like a closing-time drunk.

Nothing is black and white (except the photographs of that period), and my memories of those days are not all bad, even though there was not much to go around in the Elder Street tenement we called home. Years of war and neglect, as well as the homecoming of hundreds of thousands of soldiers, meant that we were lucky to have a room of our own at all in the despondent and overcrowded city. Fruit and meat, and clothes and paper were almost unobtainable to ordinary people, except through a flourishing black market if and when you had the money.

Our bed was a family bed in an alcove. I remember hearing my mother whispering to my father, "Your feet are like ice," and (after my brother Robert appeared in our lives) "Don't wake the baby boy." Robert slept in the bottom dresser drawer beside us, his cumulus breath meeting ours low above the cracked linoleum and cabbage roses wallpaper.

In this, my first landscape, my mother danced and wept, my dad sang and raged. In that home the mice skittered around day and night. I was used to hearing their stubborn claws under the sink, shredding the yellow newspapers that claimed we won the war. Being poor didn't seem that bad. Luxuries were a pair of nylons for my mother, a decent pair of shoes for my father, and an orange in my Christmas stocking for me. Happiness, fortunately, was deliciously democratic, and even as a child I knew what it tasted like – once, of course, the tough and bitter peel was removed. I felt safe in that place of my childhood. For what seemed the longest time it was the only home and the only life I knew, and I belonged there.

I had no rich uncles. Most, but not all, of my uncles drank too much, sang songs, danced to big band music, told jokes – which I later discovered were sexist and racist – and passed out, pleased with themselves. Most of them went to school only until age fourteen, when they could start their apprenticeships. Like my father, most of my uncles worked hard at the shipyards. They were skilled and took pride in their trades. My aunts' stories about them are epic. Ask my Aunt Joan about the day my Uncle Ronnie got married. She'll tell you that by the end of it all the women and children were barricaded behind the kitchen door against which my drunken grandfather was hurling his body, trying to get his hands on my Nanny Gloud's throat and cursing God for the day he was born and the rest of us as well.

Although family parties often seemed to end on a down note, with women and children crying, we kept having them and life went on. You'd forget.

My paternal grandmother Martha Macleod, whom we called Nanny Gloud, slipped books to me as if she were placing a bet. The first was Louisa May Alcott's *Little Women*, Christmas 1955. The second was *Jane Eyre*, Christmas 1956. Aunt Ada made me pretty frocks, Aunt Mary took care of my mother if she got sick or pregnant, and Aunt Joan, younger than the others, sang the beautiful "Tennessee Waltz" to me. My uncles gave their weekly pay packs to their wives, who did all the work at home, as well as sometimes working in the shipyards, factories, or shops. The men went to the dog track or football matches on Saturdays and owned one suit – for weddings and funerals. They told the same stories over and over. We encouraged them to do this because they told their stories so well.

Surviving the war was the top story. As I listened to the tales of the bombs dropping and exploding I imagined the helpless tenement windows, like eyes of shattering glass, lit up from behind by fire. Although they read the newspaper every day and listened to the wireless, my uncles rarely read books. Ours was an oral culture. My uncles never read Dr. Spock. They disciplined children with a belt on the side of the head – something they would never get away with now, I hope. To them, if you couldn't say everything you needed to say in words, and quickly, you would be considered illiterate. They were magicians with language in all its non-written forms – conversation, patter, the joke, the punch-line, the silence, the wink, the raised eyebrow, the subversive smile, the tear, the raised voice, the lowered eyes, the curse, the fist to the table that shakes the teacup in its saucer.

My uncles liked fried bread and blood pudding, bacon and eggs, porridge oats, fish and chips in newspaper, hot peas in vinegar, and Spam sandwiches. Lettuce was for rabbits. They loved their mothers and feared their fathers' tempers. When they were happy, they got drunk to celebrate. When they were angry, they got drunk to protest. They respected authority – doctors, teachers, priests, or ministers – but not too much. They enjoyed outwitting the police. As a child I would hear a heavy knock at the door. My grandmother would whisper, "It's the polis."

Although my uncles could be violent and angry – most of them spent at least one or two nights in jail for street fighting – they were sentimental, affectionate, and humble – in a boastful way, if that's possible. I loved them, each and every one. It was there, in the warmth of that extended family, in that war-torn place, in those austere and wonderful times, at age five that I first became aware of myself as a person, as an individual cultural and spiritual being.

◇

Sometimes on Saturday afternoons my father, who was a Protestant, would take me to a movie or to the Glasgow Art Gallery. Always on Sundays my mother, who was Catholic, would take me to mass at St. Anthony's.

The fact that my mother and father married, I later learned, was a cultural anomaly of major proportions. He married "down." Blue Protestants and green Catholics were at war with each other on the streets of Glasgow. This war was ritualized on the football fields when the Protestant Rangers played the Catholic Celtics. On the street, it was as arbitrary as any religious war.

Since my father had agreed to raise his children in the Catholic Church in order to obtain my mother's hand, I attended St. Constantine's School. On a good day I could walk to school unassailed by "proddy dog" gangs. On a bad day stones would be thrown, punches would land, and names would fly. But I could give as good as I got. "Sticks and stones/ can break my bones/ but names can never hurt me." I learned to run fast, and it seemed my knees were always scabbed. The scabs were my medals for climbing, or escaping, or finding new routes to school, sneaking through the backs and "dreeping" over washhouse walls, which we called "dykes." Of course, if I was with a gang of Catholic children, it would be the isolated Protestant school child who would have the bad day, and it would be that child who would shout the same ditty. Being a religious warrior was as natural as picking my nose or biting my nails.

I can still remember the sense of raw terror of the sea I felt while watching the film *Moby Dick*, and the awe and Catholic validation I experienced during the religious epic *The Robe*. I didn't know that Jesus Christ was a Jew, and not just a Catholic. Moreover, even though Glasgow had a large Jewish population, that part of the city and its culture was invisible to me and, I guess, others like me; I didn't even know what a Jew was until I moved to Toronto in the late 1960s.

The moment that has stayed with me and probably shaped me most as a child took place, not in school, not at home, not at St. Anthony's, and not in a movie house. It happened at the Glasgow Art Gallery when I was about five years old. That moment I call Salvador Dali, after the painter. The particular painting was called "Christ of St. John of the Cross." The angle of Christ's head and body was completely wrong. I was used to the little stick Christ that trailed on the tail of my rosary beads, or the gaudy plaster versions I saw in chapel, with painted red blood in the nail wounds. This Christ was a real man. I was looking at him from above and he was tilting towards me at the same time, his body hanging forward, in the dark in a most alarming manner. The nails were invisible. With his head bent forward, his face, of course, was hidden. He had lovely, curly, short, brown hair. His poor arms were stretched over the bar of a cross that looked like it was engineered of iron or steel. I could see every muscle in his arms, on his shoulders, on his neck. This crucified son of God was man, not icon. He was a beautiful man – just like my father. In that moment I became a preposterously devout Catholic.

"Perspective," my father said. "It's a painting about perspective," as he eventually pulled me away down the long corridors and through the other rooms in the gallery. It would be many years before I learned what perspective meant. It would be longer still before I learned about the poetry and philosophy of St. John of the Cross and his long dark night, and even longer still before I learned about a different kind of perspective – women's. John's mentor was St. Teresa of Avila, another of those women who got shut out of history. Teresa founded the Carmelite order of nuns in the twelfth century. Her common sense, hard work, organizational skills, and trust in providence became legendary. In choosing women for her spiritual team, she looked for intelligence and good judgement. Teresa believed that people who used their heads could see their faults and grow, while the narrow-minded never learned.

I remember, as my father dragged me out of the Glasgow Art Gallery that day, pointing to little framed pencil sketches and announcing, "I could do that." My father laughed and told me I couldn't. It never occurred to him that working-class women could become artists. Thirty years later, in a gallery on Queen St. in Toronto, a series of my photographs appeared in a group show called "Women's Perspective." I called them "Kitchen Sink Dramas," pictures of sinks, rubber gloves, and dishwashing liquid, presented as wedding anniversary greeting cards.

◇

When I was about six years old, in 1954, we were moved from the familiar old sandstone tenements in the heart of the city to a new housing scheme in a northwestern suburb called Drumchapel. More than a hundred thousand homes in the Glasgow core had been condemned as uninhabitable. Drumchapel, however, was uninhabitable in its own way. It was a refugee camp of sorts – a bleak wasteland it seemed to me – amidst fields of bluebells and buttercups and sheep, with no pub for my father and no schools, churches, shops, movie houses, art galleries, or dance halls.

But at least the new apartment we were assigned to had no noticeable mice and did have two bedrooms, as well as a kitchen, living room, and bathroom, with hot and cold running water that we didn't have to share with anyone.

Because of the shortage of schools, the authorities arranged for buses to take some of the children into the city's schools. I was sent to a posh all-girls Catholic School in Clydebank, in a beautiful and prosperous neighbourhood the likes of which I had never seen in Glasgow. The school was attached to the convent of Notre Dame, and the Sisters were strict. They spoke differently than I did, using "proper English," and their manners were different, too.

The Drumchapel types, like me, wore different uniforms from the other students. I wore a grey pleated skirt, a white shirt, and a royal blue blazer with a tie that matched. At the time I couldn't quite put any of this into words but I suddenly felt ugly and dirty. It was my first personal encounter with the class divide. The other girls, the girls who seemed to belong, wore trim and flattering black uniforms. They walked with their heads up, laughing. They had friends. They knew each other. They didn't bite their nails, and didn't have scabs on their knees.

I picked up on the new manners and language quickly, however, and soon worked it into an act that allowed me to become part of the regular Sunday night entertainment at Nanny Gloud's. At first my mother would have to coax me to stand in the middle of the living room and recite something I had learned in school, but it wasn't long before I couldn't wait for the meal to be over and the show to begin. To get their attention, and for effect, I'd do something like start by talking in our own dialect. "I beg your parrdon," I'd say, exaggerating the rolling of my r's. "I've somethin' good tae say, but it's harrd tae talk we ye all blethering." I would wait until my audience put down their playing cards or knitting to begin.

"*When I no more behold thee/ think on me!/ By all thine eyes have told me, think on me! When hearts are lightest/ when eyes are brightest/ when griefs are slightest/ think on me.*"

Barely understood, words like these, words I had learned off by heart, would tumble from my mouth, perfectly clipped and precise. There were lovely "ings" at the end of words, where they were meant to be. And the letter "t" would stand at attention in the middle of words, like a soldier, like it was supposed to. The words of a poem had the power to raise my chin from my chest, straighten my back, brighten my eyes, and push some bold and confident me out of my usually shy and awkward body. Thus transformed and made beautiful again by the adopted sentiments of a dead poet, I would march on:

"*When thou hast none to cheer thee, think on me!/ When no fond heart is near thee, think on me!/ When lonely sighing, / O'er pleasures flying, / when hope is dying,*" – I would pause before delivering the last line – "*Think on me!*" Curtsy. Silence. A tear would be wiped away by the back of a hand. Then applause. I was hooked.

My Uncle Ronnie would sometimes follow me with his version of the hit song "High Noon." Tapping out the rhythm ominously on the table and trying to imitate an American cowboy accent, he'd sing, "*Do not for-rrsake me, oh mah dar lin'/ on this ourrr weddin' daa aay . . .*" And sometimes it would be my father, down on one knee in front of Nanny Gloud, arms outstretched, belting out his version of Al Jolson's "Mammy." "*I'd walk a millyun miles / for one oe yer smiles / my ma am my.*" I was acquiring the best tools I could have for getting out of the working-class – language and showmanship. And although I didn't know it then, my father and my uncle were, at the same time, planning our "escape," preparing to leave Scotland for America. They really wanted out.

Away from the safety and security of my family, however, I was far from comfortable in my new school, and started to pick up another skill that I would need in my long trek towards acceptability: pretending. Pretending is not the same as telling lies. Pretending is acting. It's acting like nothing hurts, or that nothing matters, or that you know what you are doing when you don't, or that you know what people are talking about when you actually don't have a clue. It's acting like you matter, when everything around seems to say you don't. It's a first step towards the politics of recognition. It's armour, it's a shield. It turns you into a fighter. Acting takes time and practice, and had there been a box office my first foray into the craft would have been a flop.

There was no clock in our classroom, but there was a big one outside in the hallway. Once or twice a day the teacher would ask someone, usually one of the lovely girls in the black uniforms, to go to the hall, find out the time and report back. It was a special task – an honour – and I wanted the assignment so badly I was bursting. One day I shot my hand up and volunteered.

I didn't know how to tell time, but I had it figured out how I was going to handle that little problem. Someone was bound to walk by, and I would just ask them to tell me what time it was. It would be easy. Then I could skip back to the classroom, make my report, and get all the credit. Nobody would be any the wiser. Unfortunately for me, though, on that particular day nobody else appeared in the corridor. I could see the face of the clock, the big hand and the little hand. I could read the individual numbers, but I couldn't break the code. So I waited. The clock ticked away. From some far corner of the convent I could hear the unearthly Gregorian chanting of the nuns at choir practice. My face started to burn.

I could see a solitary nun on her knees scrubbing the stone floor far away, down another corridor. But I knew she wouldn't be allowed to speak to me. On that day, in those minutes, there was only me and that big unfathomable clock left on the face of the earth. My palms got all sweaty. And I waited. I could smell the aroma of boiled peas from the kitchen, so I knew it was nearly lunchtime. Eventually my teacher came to fetch me and marched me back into the classroom. I dragged my shame like a new-found weight behind me, and vowed to become a better actor.

◇

In 1957 we joined the thousands of refugees who applied for and were granted landed immigrant status in Canada. To get the money to purchase our air tickets, my mother sold a new TV set, a shiny hi-fi, a fairly decent collection of contemporary records, including Bill Haley's "Rock around the Clock," a good Hoover vacuum cleaner, a matching set of living room furniture, two bedroom suites, a kitchen table and chairs, as well as numerous knick-knacks and curtains and carpets. One thing she didn't sell was a plaster statue of St. Teresa, one that she had bought from a travelling salesman who knocked on our Drumchapel door one day. My mother packed St. Teresa carefully and carried her in our suitcases to the new life. Today, as I write these words, my mother has been dead for over ten years, and although Teresa's black veil is chipped and she certainly looks less for the wear in her brown and cream coloured Carmelite habit, she still stands watch over me.

I kissed both my grandmothers and all my aunts and uncles good-bye and headed for the new country. I wore a new Panama hat and we flew BOAC. It was my first time in an airplane.

When Ralph Glasser left Glasgow, one of his workmates warned: "Apart frae anything else it's a gey different wurrld ye'll be goin' intae. Well-to-do fellers frae hames where naebody ever wanted fer anything! Wi' different ways and ideas. Yew're no' goin' tae understand them an' they're no' goin' tae understand ye! Or I should say, won't go out of their ways tae understand ye!"

Never again would I see Nanny Gloud working in her little house on Tweedsmuir Road with her hair in combs – cooking, cleaning, sorting, carrying, sewing, darning, ironing, washing, comforting, fighting, her fist punching the air in an attempt to bring order to what was often chaos. Never again would I get to remove the combs and brush her long white hair on Sunday evenings, after the family meal had been eaten and the grown-ups were playing cards and singing songs, the coal fire lighting our spirits and keeping us one.

2

"Canada Good Country"

*On our farm in Canada, there was a chestnut tree that someone
had planted behind the barn. Every year my father threatened to
cut it down, because in all our time on the farm it had never once
produced any flowers or fruit. But finally one spring, already
long after you'd left us, it sent out a profusion of small white
buds that turned to nuts in the fall. It was as if the tree had
understood how tenuous its existence was, and had gathered up
all its resources to hold out to us this offering, this bit of hope.*

*She would have asked, Was there really a tree? Did it happen
that way? And I would have said, That was one way it could
have happened. And the yes and the no, the precision things took
on in the plain world, would not have mattered so much, only the
story, that bit of hope.*

Nino Ricci, Where She Has Gone (1997)

WE ARRIVED IN THE LAND of milk and honey at Malton Airport, just
outside of Toronto, in the month of May 1957. Not to a golden prairie
farm, like the ones we had seen in the promotional pictures of Canada; not
to the Rocky Mountain splendours; but to a great, smoking, and bustling
industrial wonderland.

My father had preceded us to Canada by a few months, sending for us
the very day – April Fool's Day, he would always remind us – that he

secured a job as a millwright at the Stelco plant in Hamilton. When we got off the plane everything was vibrating and in technicolour, so unlike the coal black and cool white of the Glasgow spring we had left behind. The air shimmered. In the arrivals lounge sunlight blinded us as we searched for my father among the eager faces and waving arms. As fellow travellers collapsed into waiting arms and were whisked away to their destinations by weeping and laughing relatives, I stood there with my shaking mother, my brother, and baby sister Janis.

A public-address-system voice like God's summoned us to a desk, and when we finally managed to find it we were reunited with my father. He had come to the airport with a friend who drove us out and away and eventually along the magnificent Queen Elizabeth Way in a brand-new brown, beige, and chrome-encrusted angel-winged Plymouth.

You will have to trust what I tell you about these early times in the life of my family because there is no written record of many of the things I talk about. You could ask me to show you the passports, the immigration papers, and the tickets. You could ask me to show you a receipt for the rent we paid to live in a couple of rooms in a family's home on Community Beach Road, just outside of the City of Hamilton. You could even demand that I supply photographs, stamped by a notary public, to prove that we did indeed live in that small, pleasant house, on a short dead-end street that led to Lake Ontario. In the month of May the beach was blanketed with delicate fish skeletons. Perhaps they were smelt.

This account of my life story is, in part, an effort to make the history of my family visible, to make it what James Hillman calls "a displayed phenomenon." All I am able to offer you is memory and the caution that if you ask my brother or my sister, they might very well tell you something completely different. They may not remember that beach, or the mosquitoes, or the rows of ants that marched through our first Canadian kitchen. If you asked my mother, she would remember the ants and the mosquitoes. She was allergic to mosquito bites, and that first summer in Canada her legs swelled up "like an elephant's."

My brother might remember the big cartons of cold orange juice, or the Popsicles, or the glass bottles of Coca-Cola that we could buy for a dime at the gas station just up the road, away from the beach. Inside the gas station, we could slide the cool top of a green bottle along one of a row of narrow rails that ran above a big red tank of ice-cold water. We could lead the bottle to the exit, then pull it free. When we popped the cap in the built-in bottle opener, the cap would drop with a muted clink into the cap collector. It was a summer, mid-afternoon outing for us in the land where things went better with Coke, Maxwell coffee was good to the very last drop, and only her hairdresser knew for sure.

My father might remember looking for a home of our own in Hamilton. He might be able to tell you what it was like answering apartment ads in the *Hamilton Spectator*, only to be told that children weren't welcome. "Adults only." We ended up moving into a trailer park, but I don't know why, exactly. Probably it was the only good place my father could find for the money he had.

Canadians called us "DPs" – displaced persons. We were a ragtag bunch of immigrants who talked funny. Real Canadians, it seemed, lived in houses. For what seemed the longest time, we lived in that rusty trailer. My mother was never as happy about our dislocation as was my father. Neither was my little sister Janis nor my brother Robert, ruptured as we were from our comfortable, state-owned, Drumchapel apartment and our large extended family. Now here we were, in a dusty trailer park in Fruitland, Ontario, in what seemed like the middle of nowhere.

Canada I discovered to be a strange new society. Inequality existed, as it did in Glasgow, but here nobody admitted the existence of boundaries between the classes. The class divisions I had encountered in Scotland always served me well as guides and road maps of sorts. If you obeyed the signals, you were all right. Class divisions in Canada were more treacherous. It was like being in a hall of mirrors on a fairgrounds midway. In these distorted, peculiar Canadian mirrors I appeared as someone even uglier, smaller, and sadder than what I felt myself to be. Soon the image of the poorly dressed and misshapen young girl in the mirror would get to me. Beyond the confines of the trailer park I could see tangible signs of affluence. I rubbed shoulders with so many other young girls who, like the black-uniformed girls in Clydebank, seemed so much more beautiful and confident. Even the milk bottles in Canada were bigger. There were huge television sets in every living room and, it seemed, in every trailer.

In our early years in Canada my father would laugh and say, "Canada good country," in his version of a first-generation Italian-Canadian accent. He would say this sitting in the one-room trailer, amidst the tattered furniture. The trailer was about twenty-four feet long and ten feet wide, and it sat stoically in a sand lot. The communal toilets and showers were a three-minute walk from the door. As for me, I sided with my father, as usual. Canada was the good life, whether we really liked it or not. Like my father I was determined to make the best of it.

Before we got our own television, my brother and I would slip out on moist summer nights to perch ourselves on a neighbour's trailer hitch and watch *The Ed Sullivan Show*, *I Love Lucy*, or whatever the Turners were watching, all to the sound of crickets. If the neighbours knew our faces were pressed against their window, they never let on. I learned to cook on a two-burner hot plate and to take care of both my mother (who was, I later realized, severely depressed) and my little sister, Janis, whose hip was accidentally fractured in a fall from a swing soon after we arrived, so that she wore a partial body cast for most of a year. In Scotland health services had been free, but at that time Canada still did not have a public health system. My sister's injury was expensive and paying the bills put my parents in debt for years. I fought with my brother, darned work socks, made beds properly, did laundry, ironed shirts, spoke Canadian, and went to school with other children who seemed to have absolutely no interest in whom I was or where I came from — except that I had a funny accent, I wore silly clothes — especially my rubber boots with the orange soles — had a face full of freckles and a severe case of acne, and I lived in the trailer park with all the poor people.

✧

Although I was easy to scare and eager to please, I soon found myself engaged in activities that would shock my parents, and, worst of all, draw unwanted attention to us.

At the front of my new school, which was called St. Francis Xavier, there was a large shrine to the Blessed Virgin. In Catholic schools feasts of the Blessed Virgin are important events, and one of the first things I noticed at this school was that it was customary for the children to bring flowers to place at the shrine on those special days. For a long time I worried about this. I had no flowers to bring. Since my father was on strike at Stelco at the time, there was no money to purchase flowers at a shop. That spring I planted hollyhock seeds and tried unsuccessfully to make a garden in the sand beside our trailer. I knew nothing about cultivating soil, fertilizing, or the important factors of sun and shade conditions on growing. Our trailer was parked on a treeless lot, and the hot sun beat down on us throughout that summer. The seeds didn't have a chance.

Then Robert came up with an idea. There was a big greenhouse operation not far from where we lived. In the fields around the greenhouses, he said, were thousands and thousands of flowers, taller than my shoulders, and in every colour of the rainbow. During our lunch break we ran through the open sunny fields and down into cool corridors of gladioli. With no time to waste, heart pounding, I knelt down and began to work a row. Keeping my head low, I started to break the strong stubborn stems with one hand and gathered as many stocks as I could hold in my free arm. Mission completed, and cradling my precious horticultural booty in both arms, I waddled on my knees to look for my accomplice.

"We better go," I whispered into the next row. Then I saw Robert was already going – crashing off through the gladioli rows, heading for the trailer park, flower stocks shooting like multicoloured rockets into the air behind him. In the same split second I saw the silhouette of a giant farmer standing above me, the sun behind him blinding me so all I could see were giant hands on his hips. I dropped the gladioli and took off after my brother. That afternoon there were no flowers from our family for the Blessed Virgin, and that evening a police officer knocked on the trailer door and asked for my father. After the police officer left, my father took off his shoe and threw it at me.

My second brush with the law happened not long after. I had been befriended by Rita, a girl who also lived in the trailer park. She was a little older than me and attended the Protestant school, in another part of town, and she told me stories about the home economics room in her school. One day as we leafed through an Eaton's catalogue Rita showed me pictures of the modern electric cooking ranges, refrigerators, washing machines, and dryers that were sitting there in her school, every weekend, unused.

One Saturday afternoon, along with another budding cook, we eased ourselves into the school through an unsecured window and sneaked along the darkened hallways into the spanking clean home economics room. For what must have been one of my happiest afternoons in Canada to that point, we busied ourselves locating the ingredients and utensils for making a cake. We beat and whipped and mixed butter and flour and eggs and sugar and chocolate, just like the recipe said. We preset the oven to 350 degrees, greased a pan, and placed the pan in the oven to bake. So successful was our first kitchen adventure that we started to make it a regular Saturday ritual, until we were noticed about three weeks later by the school janitor, who was able to identify my friends. Although we escaped, the law quickly caught up with us. This time the police came to my classroom and I was called out into the hall for questioning. "Whatever possessed you?" my teacher asked. "Of course, your father will have to be told." I was the first one in our family to make it into a newspaper story. *The Hamilton Spectator* ran a little piece about us under a headline that announced: "Cake Loving Trio Nabbed in School."

I had no name for what was happening to me in those days. What I know now is that any confidence and sense of well-being that had been growing in me as a child in Scotland was slowly replaced by an oppressive sense of myself as an outsider, a sinner, and a criminal at that. No matter how deeply I slept, how sweetly I dreamt in the days and weeks following that newspaper story, there was not a morning I awoke without remembering the headline, without feeling my heart sink, and without fanning the flames of shame I had invited into my father's house. Our hybrid working-class, Catholic and Protestant culture was solidly based on a sense of shame. Because my father had promised that his children would be raised Catholic, it was the Catholic thinking that dominated my early experiences and learning. But it was a particular type of Catholicism. My well-intentioned mother and my teachers carried and passed on to me a version of "The Faith" that taught that the human body was corrupt, salvation was not universal, and God was to be feared. God was the policeman at my door. It was a doctrine of absolute predestination. From the word go, everyone was destined to be either saved or damned, and only a chosen few would enter the kingdom of heaven. This God was unlike the beautiful one I had seen in the Salvador Dali painting at the Glasgow Art Gallery. This God was an unyielding judge who was raising a heavy gavel above my head, ready to hammer down His verdict of guilty.

The problem was I was guilty not only of spiritual transgressions but also of being poor. It was obvious to me in the clothes I wore and the shyness that stole my tongue that we lived in poverty. This must be my punishment for my sins. I knew that if I wanted God to be a friend of mine, if I wanted to be one of the chosen few, and one day own more than one pair of shoes, I would have to clean up my act. Fast. I had several major counts against me, but if I did penance, perhaps I stood a chance. I knew that the nature of my sins — being of the venial and not mortal type — did not warrant damnation to hell, but I was pretty sure that I was not heaven material either. I would have to spend a good deal of time in the waiting room first, the place we called purgatory. At the same time, from what I understood about my religion, all these discomforts and disadvantages could be put to good use – I could offer them up as sacrifices to atone for those same sins. But what about my Protestant father?

It was around that time that I began to have a recurring nightmare in which I carried the dead body of my father on my shoulders. I was always on the same gas-lit street, lined on both sides by closed and darkened doorways. I would knock on one door and then another, asking that my father be accepted for burial. But no one would accept his body. Though I was in a state of anxiety in the dream, my father was laughing. He was not nearly as worried as I was about getting into heaven. He didn't seem to care.

Someday I will go to the microfilm records of *The Hamilton Spectator* and search through back issues for a photograph taken in 1959. It was a shot of my parents, with Janis on my father's knee, taken in the trailer during the strike that turned my father from a skilled trades worker at Stelco into a fruit picker. To help stretch the strike pay he went out to work in the orchards near St. Catharines. The photo offers up one of those images that newspapers like to run "to put a human face" on the stories of the day. I have said that this part of the story must depend on my memory. Another memory of that strike comes from a black and white photograph of the time, and I vividly remember the missing colours: my yellow hula hoop, my brown and white saddle shoes, my pink T-shirt, and the red cherries that grew in the trees of temptation outside the confines of the trailer park.

3

Skating on Thin Ice

Out here I am like someone without a sheet
without a branch but not even safe as the sea,
without the relief of the sky or good graces of a door.
If I am peaceful in this discontent, is not peace,
is getting used to harm . . .

Dionne Brand, *Land to Light On* (1997)

BY DECEMBER 1962 we were deep in Petawawa, about 160 kilometres north of Ottawa. In our new home, from a mattress on the floor that I shared with my brother and sister, I could raise my arm and reach the frozen window with my left hand. If I placed my hand flat against the window and held it there until the cold entered my body and the frost cleared from the pane, I could create my own hand-shaped lens through which to see the world outside.

At that window I discovered the meaning of cold. A village sleeping on the banks of the Ottawa River on a 40 below zero (Fahrenheit) night. A mongrel slipping across a luminous snowcrust. Naked shrubs grabbing and letting go, cringing then relaxing. A wind, the like of which I had never heard before. I could also make out the sleek outline of my father's 1949 Pontiac, plugged in so it would be ready for his morning drive to work. Beyond the car I could make out the shape of Our Lady of Sorrows

Church. Beyond the church, and hidden from my view, was the new school I attended, which bore the same name as the church. Far beyond my sight, out in the bush, rabbits struggled and died in the silver snares my father had learned to set. For he was now catching food for the family. In the night I could still hear my father snoring. I knew his lunch bucket was sitting on the table ready for him when he woke up, his green parka hung on the coat hook like a soldier at a urinal.

On my birth certificate my father's occupation is listed as "pipefitter." In Petawawa, though, he was something different, a "millwright." He had a job at the fairly new atomic energy plant in nearby Chalk River. Since radioactive fuel rods didn't seem to frighten him, why should I have been worried? Back then, nobody told me anything. All I knew was that Chalk River was up the road, my father had a job there, and just what was going on in that kind of work was not discussed in school. How was I to know that Canada had helped to usher in the atomic age in 1945? Chalk River had been chosen as the site of Canada's first nuclear reactor and the facility was up and running in September 1945, a month after two U.S. atomic bombs had been dropped on Japan. Atomic energy was all the rage after the war, and in 1952 Atomic Energy of Canada Limited, a Crown corporation, was created to develop its "peaceful uses."

Petawawa itself had a large military base – a place that was booming in an era of rapidly increasing defence expenditures encouraged by the Korean and Cold wars. My father would drive past the base each morning on his way up Highway 17 to the Atomic Energy of Canada plant in Chalk River. For my father the power of the great ships of the Glasgow yards, which used to fill him with immense pride, a pride he passed on to me during our visits to the marine museum in Glasgow – was nothing compared to the new job. My father, like most other people at the time, believed that nuclear power was the greatest thing since electric pop-up toasters. The development of nuclear energy, he said, was the most brilliant thing the world had ever seen. Nuclear science was bigger than life. Its power was ultimate.

I recall those Petawawa nights of moon time and breathing, for part of me has never left that place of open eyes and sleeplessness. I still carry within me that cold rented house, our first house in Canada, with its linoleum floor walked thin and pale by previous tenants. There were five bedrooms, and at night all of them were empty, because we crowded into the only room we could afford to heat with our one small space heater. We were used to being close together.

Again, there was no running water. There was indoor plumbing and a bathroom with a pink bathtub, a sink, and a toilet, but the water was not hooked up. We learned to use an outhouse, a short twenty steps out the back door. There was also a bucket we could use, if necessary. I can still smell the scents of oil smoke, Detol, urine, and Vicks Vapo-rub.

My brother slept with hockey cards under his pillow. Late at night, after the lights were turned out, I could read my books by the moonlight and the streetlights. And I feared the morning and going to school. My mother would push me out the door.

At school that December I was the new girl, the new game, the hat-less and bare-legged outsider. I was the "other" who – to be initiated into my new life – was required to run the length of a jeering gauntlet my schoolmates formed. In the weekday mornings dozens of children – strangers to me for what seemed the longest time – packed and hidden in grey nylon snowsuits, would congregate in the yard of Our Lady of Sorrows School, a snowball toss from our house. I could see the pupils arriving – walking and running in twos and threes or tumbling out of the slush-covered school buses that steamed into the yard like yellow tanks. They would blow into their mitts and stamp their feet on packed snow. As I walked towards the crowd, its noise grew and thickened. It pushed. It kicked. It shoved. The game would end and the group would disperse only when I fell or cried, or when the bell rang. One morning blood dripped from my nose and froze into a perfect red rose in the snow. I picked up the lump with care and defiantly put it in my pocket.

I don't believe Sister Ursula enjoyed teaching. I know that inside the school, on the warm side of the door just beside the statue of the Sacred Heart, she would balance herself on her toes while the bell rang, then rock back on her heels. Outside, as we fell into line, prepared to go in, we would see her throw the door open as if to release her heart and let all the kindness she possessed fly from her face like a bird. We would march past her in dutiful pairs, honouring the authority of her professional stone face either by avoiding her eyes or attempting modest nods. We would wind into the cloakroom to kick off our boots. From the corner of my eye – for I dared not look at them directly for fear of drawing more heat – I would see my tormentors slip out of their snowsuits, like soldiers after battle preparing for sleep.

A copy of a book on the life of Dr. Tom Dooley sat on top of the Baltimore edition of the catechism on Sister Ursula's battleship grey desk. Behind her desk was a green blackboard. On the wall to the right of the desk was a map of the world, the communist countries clearly highlighted. Also, to the right of her desk was a wall of windows, decorated with poster paint to herald the beginning of the Christmas season. All the eyes painted on the window mural were sky blue and perfectly round.

The Three Wise Men sat on their brown camels, seeming to lurch and sway towards a five-point primary yellow star. Beneath the star were a stable, a man in brown, a woman in blue, and a baby in bright, flesh pink. Each had yellow halos painted around their heads, the same yellow as the star. White angel hair, sprinkled with sparkles, unravelled as snow along the full length of the sill.

In the corner by the sink at the back of the room, the paint brushes sat in clean jam jars. Beside the paint brushes were several white rabbit skins, props for the nativity play we would be preparing for the Christmas concert. Apparently Sister Ursula had taught the Christmas story in this way for nearly thirty years in her Ottawa Valley classrooms. This particular year she was determined to finish, before the Christmas holidays, the story of Dr. Dooley's trials in Laos, at the hands of the merciless Communists.

Tom Dooley, she told us, was a good Catholic doctor who was captured by Communists and hung from a tree in a cage in the sweltering sun. Bamboo shoots were driven into his fingers, underneath his nails. Would he renounce his faith, this saint of a man – beaten and humiliated by beasts in a faraway country? It was important for us to know what Communists did to Catholics, but, while it was important for us to know what Catholicism was – we had daily and rigorous catechism drills – it was not important for us to know what Communism was. All we needed to know about Communism was that it meant torture for good Catholics like Dr. Dooley.

One morning a snow plough thundered by, shaking the crucifix on the wall beside the clock. A sparkling blanket of ice-covered snow slid slowly off the roof of a cheerless grey Insulbrick house across the road. It landed with a silent thud. Beside me, a classmate – overwhelmed by the details of torture – slumped in a faint to the floor, her face ash white. She had to be carried from the room. Why a little Canadian nun in Petawawa, Ontario, was reading to her students from *Deliver Us from Evil* is beyond me today. The foreword states that Dr. Tom Dooley "contributed greatly to the welfare of mankind and to a fundamental understanding of the United States. ... It is a story that will be told and retold. It is a story of which the United States Navy is proud."

I still carry three other things with me from Petawawa. The most significant, I suppose, is losing the Carnival Queen competition. Second is my first official foray into show business, in the coveted role of the Blessed Virgin in the "Huron Christmas Carol" nativity pageant we performed in the church basement that winter. The third is winning the Lion's Club public-speaking competition.

To compete in the Carnival Queen competition I had to learn to skate. Certainly, to make myself into a Canadian I had to learn. So when charitable neighbours gave me a pair of used tube skates, I pulled them on and went to work at the outdoor community rink. The cold toes, sore ankles, bruised knees, shaky legs, and cramped arches soon gave way to my efforts of inching along the boards, then gliding along with my legs stiff and knees together. Soon I could remain upright for long periods of time. Then I was actually turning corners, rather than banging into the end of the rink. Head up, wind in my face, snowflakes landing on my nose, moving in harmony with my competition. Keeping up. No doubt wiping my runny nose on my coat sleeve. Fast boys weaving in and out of the crowd, scaring us, daring us. Strauss waltzes blaring over an old public address system, under a string of magic light bulbs. I am finally free and for the first time I feel the power of grace. The music is inside of me. Racing then, finally, stopping on a dime. My arms raised high above my head. The smell and crackle of the fire burning in a rusty oil drum where we warm our hands, while the scrap of shovels clears the rink again. Hot chocolate. Can this Canadian girl be me?

By the time the Winter Carnival rolled around I had the confidence to enter the Carnival Queen competition. Alongside the rink the village fathers installed tin cans bearing the names of the competitors. Spectators voted for the queen by dropping coins in the can of their favourite. I think I came in last, or at least it felt that way when the vote was counted and the third, second, and first prize winners were announced, and my name was not to be heard. Encouraged by my father to get out there and do my best, and having done exactly as I was told, I had not realized the disadvantage of being the new girl in town. With no extended network of family and friends to back me, I didn't stand a chance. It was (to say the least) a wrenching initiation into the world of formal politics. I was completely surprised by the humiliation. It wasn't fair. My father tried to comfort me, but I was inconsolable for days.

If it had not been for the Christmas pageant, I would probably have fallen off the face of the earth. I was the one picked to wear a fur coat of sorts with a blue veil and hold a doll wrapped up in rabbit skins while the rest of my classmates sang the words to the beautiful Huron Christmas carol: "*T'was in the moon of winter time, when all the birds had fled/ The Mighty Gitchi Manitou sent angel choirs instead.*" Were there drums beating? Was the usually cheerless church basement hall really hushed and sacred and glorious? Was I actually holding the symbol of God's love for us in my arms? Was I its mother?

But it was the Lion's Club Public Speaking Competition that really cheered me up. "Madam Chairman, ladies and gentlemen, girls and boys," I began, a few weeks later in the same church hall, packed with parents, students, and all the local politicians and businessmen. I was on a roll. I talked about the effects of automation, pointing dramatically to a thermostat on the wall that controlled the furnace, and I explained how automatic potato pickers in Prince Edward Island were making unnecessary cuts in the potatoes we now buy in the shops. I must have made a convincing argument and presented it forcefully because I walked away with the second prize cup, which I still have, although the arms have been missing for years. A tall boy, whose speech I have completely forgotten, came first.

When I look back on those years, I wonder why no one talked about nuclear power. In Glasgow, everybody talked about ships. Launchings of new ships were festive events, and when the ship industry died everybody mourned in public. In Petawawa the entire economy of the community was tied up in the Chalk River reactors and the military base. But these topics were not on the Lion's Club public-speaking list.

One of the things I learned in Petawawa was that the church could be a safe place in the midst of adversity. I began to attend morning mass each day before school, and after mass was over I would sit for a while in the empty, silent church. Alone with the candles, the statues, and the Stations of the Cross, I could pray on my own for my salvation and some kind of sign. Literally minded about my religion, I wanted the statues to move or wink. I had learned about a point system called "indulgences," whereby certain prayers and activities, like singing in the choir, could be used to accumulate points. These points, in turn, could be applied to reduce the time I would have to spend in purgatory. So I believed that my time was being put to good use and I came to love Gregorian chants and particularly the music for the requiem mass. When I heard the school bell ring I had enough time to run and take my place in line. In this way I managed to replace the humiliation of the gauntlet with a new-found sense of holiness. I became the girl who went to mass every single day.

And lo and behold, within a year my prayers were answered and things began to change. The taunts began to fade. I made new friends, the teachers liked me, and my marks soared. Most significantly, my parents were able to buy a new house. The sign on the highway, just south of the village on the way to Pembroke, said, "Pine Meadows. Three-bedroom ranch-style bungalows. $500 down." We packed up again and moved into the new house, and this time it looked like my father's big gamble might pay off – we finally had a bathroom that worked. We also had nice neighbours who needed babysitters, for there were dozens of families just like ours all around, and I was just the right age, at fifteen, to be in demand. By securing a *Toronto Star* paper route and saving my babysitting money I was soon able to buy my own clothes. I learned the fashion trends by pouring over copies of *Seventeen* magazine. My first big shopping expedition in the bargain basement of a Pembroke shop saw me decked out in a new winter coat, shoes, socks, gloves, and a hat – all in different shades of red, from tomato to scarlet.

My favourite babysitting job was looking after the three children of a teacher at the high school in the military base. Mr. Bear was the first black man I had ever met. His wife was white. After the children were asleep I was allowed to play the family's stereo, the first component system I had ever seen. Everyone else had hi-fi systems built into big pieces of furniture. This system had separate speakers, a turntable, and an amplifier with lights and knobs and buttons. Each time I came to look after the children, the Bears would show me records they thought I might like to play. At other homes where I babysat, if the parents came home late they would find me asleep on the couch. Not so at the Bears': I was always awake. It was there I first heard the startling, pure voice of Joan Baez, the protest songs of Bob Dylan, and the magic in the voice of the African singer Miriam Makeba. I started trying to imitate their songs, and my brother started playing a guitar. Everything seemed to be falling into place – I met my first boyfriend, a handsome young man named Jay who was planning to enter the priesthood. He treated me kindly, with respect. I had two "best" girlfriends, Eileen and Pat, from the same neighbourhood. I could share my innermost thoughts with them, and we could exchange books. Eileen gave me *Catcher in the Rye* by J.D. Salinger. My mother didn't approve of my friendship with Eileen. The problem was, Eileen could pick up a book and read any time and was not expected to do housework or help her mother. My mother saw this as laziness. I was only permitted to read after the housework was done. In our house there was no money for music lessons or summer camps. But it was more than the money. These things were not even considered to be important. In my high-school years, besides Salinger, I was reading William Golding, Aldous Huxley, and Harlequin Romances. After winning a memorable fight with the local librarian who liked to make sure the young people were not corrupted by what they read, I managed to get my hands on copies of Robert Service's two autobiographies, *Harper of Heaven* and *Ploughman of the Moon*. At school my marks were good in everything except math and science. I excelled in catechism. I was elected class president. I enjoyed going to Pembroke Ironmen* Junior A hockey games and cheering for the cutest players. Although I took pride in my domestic accomplishments, I began to wish I could linger longer at school and have more time to read and socialize.

Whenever we got the chance, Pat, Eileen, and I exchanged fashion tips and poured over magazines, dreaming of beauty with our hair in rollers and our faces plastered with cream. On weekends we would journey into Pembroke and make our way to the TV station, where Saturday afternoon teen dances were broadcast live and we could do the Locomotion in front of untold thousands. Shag skirts, stretch ski pants, and banlon sweater sets were in vogue. My favorite sweater set was canary yellow. We also taught

---

*Now called the "Lumber Kings," the team was called the "Ironmen" when they were sponsored by Pemco Steel.

each other how to sew and would spend hours choosing Simplicity patterns and materials to make our special outfits. I was on my knees on the living room floor, using pinking shears to cut out a pattern for a dress, the evening of the day U.S. President Kennedy was assassinated in Dallas. The fabric was a dusty-rose-coloured wool, and the unfolding television coverage of the day's tragedy dominated my thoughts. The next week at school we prayed for Kennedy's soul.

I remember family suppertime in the Petawawa house, the five of us eating in silence, our elbows on the table, absentmindedly shovelling the food into our mouths with our forks, our eyes glued to *Yogi Bear* on the television set, which we could see from the kitchen table. Most evenings after the dishes were done, with Spam sandwiches made and wrapped in wax paper for the next day, we would watch a couple more hours of television. During the evenings my mother would often set up the ironing board in the living room and work on a pile of clothes while she watched. The cycle of laundry and ironing was without end. My father would fall asleep on the couch. Since it was hard to read with the television on, I usually took my books to bed with me, in the room I shared with my sister.

We hadn't been long in the house outside Petawawa – I was in Grade 10 – when my father announced that we were moving again. He had a new job, this time in western Ontario.

4

My Father's Nuclear Dream

A society committed to purely material values cannot survive.
Most of the human family has been engaged in the universal
effort to keep body and soul together — to get enough to eat, to
keep the wrinkles out of empty bellies, to provide enough cloth-
ing to keep people from freezing and to find a minimum shelter
for the family. In the affluence that exists in North America,
the human family has the opportunity to create communities in
which everyone can grow as social, cultural and spiritual beings.

Walter Reuther, UAW (1969)

BEFORE WE MOVED to Kincardine my father showed us postcards of its
Lake Huron beach and blue sky. The harbour and the pretty white and
red lighthouse sold me on the idea of living there. It looked so safe and
peaceful. The sunsets pictured in the postcards were spectacular, as they
indeed turned out to be. When we got to Kincardine in 1963, the western Ontario town's economy was dominated by the construction of the
Bruce Nuclear Power Development, about sixteen kilometres north.
This new economy had already managed to displace over a century of
the town's industrial history. The once prominent woollen mills and
furniture factories were either gone or going. That was the past. The
work of extracting heavy water, splitting atoms, and controlling

nuclear power to produce electricity was to be the all-important task of the mysterious future.

People made a lot more money working at the plant than they had ever brought in before by building tables and chairs, harvesting crops, or sewing in a textile plant – the human-scale economy supplanted by Ontario Hydro's massive nuclear projects. Hydro workers like my father were called "Hydroids" by the locals, who saw us as alien ugly sisters cramming ourselves into their idyllic Cinderella slippers. But Hydroid dollars were more than welcome.

This time the family move seemed more like a holiday than an uprooting to another town with another school to go to, new people to meet, and new customs to learn. But I underestimated the cultural shock I would experience, once we settled. We packed the five of us, along with everything we owned, into a borrowed 1947 Chevy pick-up truck. We drove 500 kilometres without looking back – from Atomic Energy of Canada, Chalk River, to Douglas Point, Ontario Hydro, Kincardine.

To historians or archaeologists, the three decades of the Ontario Hydro plant's active life might be brief episodes, but they are my history in that town. I remember my father in front of the television reading his nuclear training manuals. His apprentice papers verified that he knew how to build ships, and, now, in the pale blue light of the television set, I watched him learn how to apply his skills to the building of a nuclear plant. As he memorized words and techniques and instructions he handed them down to me. I put them into my head along with my catechism lessons and tried, as best I could, to accommodate what seemed like two competing worldviews: Catholicism and modern science.

At the time the church was losing its hold on me, and my focus on the world around me was changing. There was no established Catholic parish in town, although there was a small church called St. Anthony's that was packed twice each Sunday when a priest visited to say mass and hear confession. Nor was there a Catholic high school. So when I began to feel the first real stirrings of my sexuality – when that mystery began to assert its complicated and delicious self — it tackled my innocence with the full force of a six-foot-four football linebacker. His name was Martin Quinn. My former sense of holiness was defenceless against the new pleasures unleashed by the impact of our budding relationship. The temptations were too great. Still, although I wanted dearly to believe that God wouldn't expect me to abstain from eating such lovely fruit, I couldn't quite convince myself that the way was clear — I knew what had happened to Eve, after all. Nor could I abstain, as much as I tried and tried. The old priest, not up to the task, could offer no guidance. Not surprisingly, he didn't attempt to tell me about the sacredness and value of my sexuality. He couldn't tell me about its power. To him sex was sin, sacramental only in marriage, and suitable only for purposes of procreation, period. He could offer no advice about how to nurture, honour, and protect my sexuality in its vulnerable emergent season.

Nor could I talk to my mother. Sex was for marriage, and as she got to know about my relationship with Martin she became determined that I should marry him. And at first I did want to marry him, but it was not to be that simple. When I became too embarrassed to confess the same sins — to tell the truth about what was happening to me — to the same anonymous priest, week after week, I stopped going to mass altogether. Having to choose between body and soul, between the material and the sacred, I voted for the body and the material. It never occurred to me to pray for both. Guilt and chaos flooded into the enormous space created when I turned my back on my faith. When I marched out of my Garden of Eden I experienced inner fear for the first time — much deeper than any of the physical fears I had already confronted.

I wasn't aware that there was such a thing as a family counsellor. I had no information about birth control. In my church, although premarital sex and birth control were both sins, out-of-wedlock pregnancies and shotgun weddings were common. A number of my schoolmates had dropped out of school to get married. They got "bad names" as a result. Others were sent away to "visit aunts" for six months, and their babies were put up for adoption. Those from moneyed families, I learned later, had abortions.

This new layer of shame led me into the first of many rounds of depression. Without any language I could use to sort out my feelings, I went to our family doctor and described the symptoms — lack of sleep, inability to concentrate on my school work, fury at my parents, and deep sense of loneliness. I had secrets I couldn't share with anyone. What I couldn't articulate was that the more I was desired by my young lover, the more my sexuality emerged in all its complicated and challenging forms, the more I hated myself. The more I hated myself, the more I hated him and anyone else who was attracted to me. The doctor prescribed Valium, and soon I was taking them like Lifesavers. Soon after that I was in the hospital, recovering from a deliberate overdose. After I got out the incident was never discussed.

I tried as best I could to cover the adventure and innocent exploration of my sexual rebellion in a costume of conformity. I learned how to roller-skate, and as soon as I turned sixteen Martin taught me how to drive his 1939 Plymouth Coupe down country roads. I played basketball, strummed chords on a twelve-string guitar, sang, drank beer, went to parties, stayed out late at night. I skipped classes at school and sunbathed on the beautiful Kincardine beach in the summer, when I wasn't working as a waitress or a dishwasher at the Sunset Restaurant. I started saving my money to go shopping in Detroit for the right clothes each August, just before school started. I was making the scene in a sharp green duffle coat, madras plaid shirts, penny loafers, burgundy sweaters, and matching knee socks. Still, nothing was quite working the right magic, or so it seemed.

I even started a folk-singing group with my brother. He played and I sang at high school functions and in Legion halls throughout Bruce County. Others joined our group, and although Robert was the only one who could tune a guitar, I enjoyed the experience of performing and the rehearsals we held at Linklater's Funeral Home. Liza, the funeral director's

My first drunk is something I have never forgotten. One Sunday afternoon my parents were out, the housework was done, and I was sitting on the floor in the living room, listening to The Mamas and the Papas sing "California Dreamin'." The music was magic, the sun was pouring in, and I was happy. I decided to try one of my father's beers. It tasted so good and went down so smoothly, I decided to try another. Soon I was feeling more than just happy. I surveyed my creative handiwork in the room. I had convinced my mother to try a Spanish decorating theme. She had permitted me to paint the side window frame in flat black and to hang red velvet curtains from a wrought iron rod. The new broadloom matched the curtain, as did the lampshades. Behind me, above the couch, was a big velvet landscape painting that I didn't much like, but I was more than pleased with the water-colour painting I had done of a long-haired, bare-footed woman in a red dress, inspired by an illustration in my Joan Baez songbook. She was holding a guitar and gazing out to sea from a cliff while below her a small boat pulled out of the harbour.

My mother had bought octagonal end tables with ornate handles. Not bad. In the corner china cabinet was my mother's collection of bowling trophies and Blue Mountain pottery. On top of the big television in the corner of the room were framed school portraits of Robert, Janis, and me.

In the days before drugs, drinking was our main recreation. Although I started drinking later than a lot of my friends, once I started there was no stopping me. Just outside town, there was a lovely farm owned by the parents of a schoolmate. Believing it better to let their teenagers drink at home rather than get killed in a drinking and driving accident, the parents allowed us to gather at their house for our weekend parties. Soon after I discovered how a few beers could make me feel remarkably strong, I was spending most Friday and Saturday nights in that warm farm kitchen, with its welcoming oil stove in the corner, worn plaid jackets and parkas hanging on hooks beside the door, and rubber boots and Kodiaks lined up along the wall. It was a kitchen big enough to hold not only the big wooden table, a couch, and many comfortable chairs but also a dozen or so local teenagers in various stages of drunkenness, bravado, and silliness.

Sometimes we would spill out of the house to play games of chicken with the electric fence. Other nights, under a big yellow summer moon, the tractor was brought from the barn for a slow ride down the soft shoulder of the highway, the sounds of laughter and daring folding behind us in the reckless dark. In that farm house we found room enough for the privacy to practise sex, which we preferred to call love. And we could use other rooms to watch television, listen to music, and dance.

It wasn't all happy times and fellowship. One night I brought my Joan Baez records out to the farm with me, thinking that my friends would like to hear something a little different from the Top 40 hits. I placed my albums on the table beside the record player and, one by one, began stacking them on the turntable. In those days you didn't worry about the finer points of musical reproduction, like records in a pile getting scratched. "*You must leave now/ take what you need/ you think will last/ but whatever you wish to keep / you better grab it fast...*" Baez sang a Bob Dylan song. Before I knew what was happening my closest girlfriend went over and scratched the needle across the record. She lifted it from the turntable, grabbed the entire stack, and began to toss them around the room like flying saucers. I tried to catch them, reaching and falling over chairs, screaming for her to stop. She was laughing. It was a game. She began to crack my precious records over her knee, tossing the pieces into the corner with the wet boots. "*It's all over now, baby blue.*" I think it wasn't just drunkenness. We'd had long talks together, she knew I was leaving town, and she was staying. Maybe she felt I was abandoning her.

My love for art, music, and poetry has always been a refuge to me. Martin, whom I loved more deeply than I could afford to admit, read my poetry and always encouraged me. I still have a beautiful book of impressionist paintings that he gave to me for Christmas 1966. It contained dozens of full-colour plates by Manet, Cezanne, Renoir, Degas, and others. The one that spoke most directly to me then was Monet's "Train Sous La Neige," which reminded me of the Kincardine train station in winter, where I often walked to see the night train pull into the station. I would count the days until I could board that train and leave forever.

I lived in Kincardine for only three years. As soon as I could, right after high-school graduation, I left my parents' home for Toronto. I left my mother.

◇

Besides the relic of my youth, there are two other relics I can see at the same time, from the same spot, on the south beach of Kincardine when I visit the shore today. One is the rusted boiler of the *Erie Belle*, a scavenger tug that sank off the shore in 1883, at the peak of Kincardine's shipping years. The second is the Douglas Point nuclear reactor.

Standing on the beach with the sun setting, if I turn my head to the right, I can see the first cool twinkles of the plant dome, off in the distance to the north. In the twilight it seems to rest there like the ghost of an ocean liner. It hums. My mother never trusted radiation, but then, she was a woman who trusted only God. After growing up and marrying merchant seaman Alex Kiltie, just as the Second World War began, she received a letter from the King telling her Alex had drowned in the Pacific Ocean. His convoy had been hit by enemy fire. She survived that tragedy and went on to marry my father. Then she lost her first baby in childbirth. Again, she survived the pain and found the strength of will to start again. She was then required to leave her Glasgow family behind and follow my father with her three children, and no money, to Canada, where, once again, she remade herself. She worked at a series of jobs – as a chamber maid, waitress, babysitter, and, finally, a ward aid in the Kincardine hospital.

When her heart finally exploded from sheer wear and tear in 1985, she was buried in the Kincardine cemetery in a grave overlooking Lake Huron. My father credited her strength to survive on her faith. She never stopped reminding me that I should have married Martin Quinn.

BUCKINGHAM PALACE

The Queen and I offer you our
heartfelt sympathy in your great
sorrow.

We pray that your country's
gratitude for a life so nobly given
in its service may bring you some
measure of consolation.

George R.I.

*Letter from the King
telling my mother,
Cathie, that her first
husband, Alex Kiltie,
had died at sea.*

*Cathie's (my mother's)
national registration card.*

Maternal grandmother Margaret Corr worked as a finisher in Glasgow's garment industry and raised seven children.
[Author's collection]

Paternal grandparents Martha and Robert Macleod. Martha slipped books to me as if she were placing a bet. Among the various jobs he held, my grandfather was a ship's purser on the Anchor line.
[Author's collection]

Bob Macleod (father) with workmates in Glasgow. [Author's collection]

Mother, Father, and baby Janis (foreground) with brother Robert and Catherine in Drumchapel, Glasgow, shortly before immigrating to Canada in 1957. [Author's collection]

Cathie Macleod with baby Janis, Hamilton, Ontario, waterfront, 1957. [Author's collection]

Workers outside Ontario Hydro's Bruce Nuclear Power Development, Douglas Point Nuclear Reactor near Kincardine, circa mid-'60s. [Photo: Ontario Hydro]

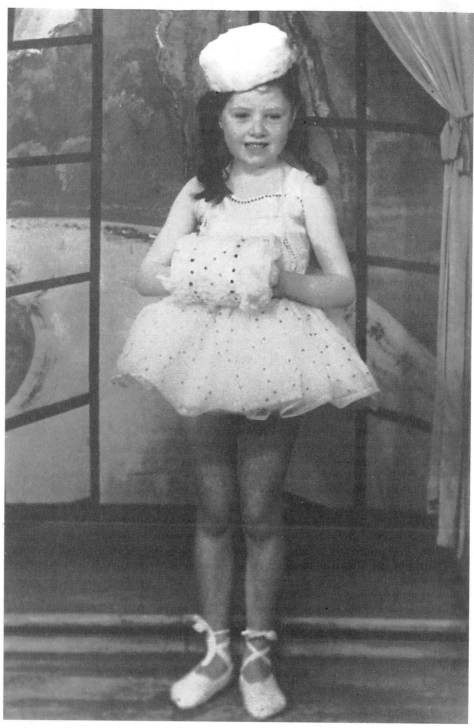

Catherine in ballet outfit. [Author's collection]

*Cathie, Robert, Catherine, and neighbour pose with the family's first car in
Canada, a 1949 Pontiac, at the trailer park in Fruitland, Ontario, in 1958.*
[Author's collection]

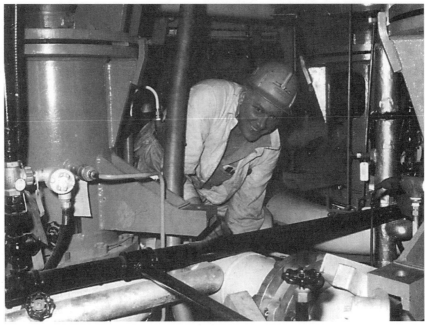

*Dad at work at Ontario Hydro's Bruce Nuclear Power Development,
near Kincardine.* [Author's collection]

Aunt Bea Macleod Hall, summer 1997. [Photo: Catherine Macleod]

Uncle Ronnie Macleod in Chapeau, Quebec. In his later years (he died in 1990) he enjoyed living in a trailer on a beautiful rented property on the Quebec side of the river, owned by Bea's daughter, Grace, and her family. [Photo: Catherine Macleod]

Martin and Catherine outside the Quinn greenhouses in Kincardine, circa 1966. [Photo: Harold Quinn]

Catherine and Andy Taylor, Hart House, University of Toronto, 1972.
[Author's collection]

Martin Quinn riding in the late, great sixties. [Photo: Tom Cuyler]

Martin Quinn canoeing in Pinery Provincial Park, 1991. [Photo: Catherine Macleod]

5

"Feed Your Head..."

I ARRIVED IN TORONTO in the summer of 1968, the year thousands and thousands of my generation, all over the world, were revolting against their parents and their countries' governments. When the United States intensified its war against Vietnam, young Americans refused to fight. It was the year of draft dodgers, sit-ins, teach-ins, mass demonstrations, and student protests. In the spring in France, students and workers led a nationwide strike. In the United States in August the "whole world" watched riot police attack antiwar demonstrators at the Democratic Party's convention in Chicago.

I slipped into the Toronto version of the brave new counterculture as easily as I slipped into the colourful, loose-fitting garments I found in Yorkville shops. Rich kids, in ragged jeans and sporting long hair, were rejecting their parents' materialistic lifestyles and values. It was a time of back to the land, drugs, brown rice, free love, peace, patchouli oil, Colombian Gold, hash pipes, and burning candles on wooden crates in darkened rooms. The tools I would use to shed my old skin were sex, acid rock, folk music, higher education, beer, Andy Warhol, Rochdale College, Ingmar Bergman films with subtitles, and all-nighters on Yorkville Avenue.

The small portfolio of paintings and drawings I had assembled was not considered good enough to get me into the Ontario College of Art, and my marks — which had dropped steadily as I fumbled my way through high school — were not good enough to qualify me for university. But I quickly landed a job at the Canada Life Assurance Company on University

Avenue, in a large grey building with a roof beacon that told the weather in flashing coloured lights. Canada Life would pay me $54 a week to sit in a room as big as a football field along with hundreds of other women and men coding computer cards. It was my job to pencil in one small box on the cards that were plunked on my desk in stacks of fifty or so held together with thick rubber bands. As soon as one batch was completed, another would arrive. Because I didn't own any business-like outfits I borrowed two cotton dresses from a friend in Kincardine. She also made me two pairs of cotton, hip-hugging bell-bottom pants, one pair white with navy-blue polka dots, the other a yellow-flowered print. And before I left town she showed me how to straighten my long hair with an iron. It seemed to me that if I squinted my eyes and looked in the mirror I did look a bit like Sylvia Tyson, my favourite Canadian folksinger.

From my Aunt Joan, who had been visiting our family from Scotland, I borrowed a pair of blue sling-back pumps with two-inch heels and a blue plastic Air Canada bag to use as my matching purse. I alternated the two dresses each day until I had enough money to buy something new for myself.

I found a furnished room for $10 a week easily enough on Spadina Avenue in a three-storey Victorian mansion owned and operated by Campus Co-op, a student-run housing service just up the road from College Street and the Silver Dollar Tavern. I unpacked my blue jeans and sweat shirts and set up house in a shared room with two pleasant world-travelling Australian sisters. Although we quickly became quite friendly, the younger of the sisters, Dana, didn't manage to tell me until late that summer that she was pregnant. Such things were still not discussed.

Meals at the co-op, included in the rent, were basic meat and potatoes and served cafeteria-style in a busy communal dining room on pastel blue or yellow or pink Melmac plates. Days in Toronto were hot that summer, and our room with its one single bed and a set of bunks was even hotter at night. Each week the members of the student management team would supply one clean sheet per bed, explaining that the top sheet was to be placed on the bottom and the fresh one on top. The father of the child Dana was carrying was one of the student managers. It was only when I made the mistake of developing a big crush on the fellow that I found out about the pregnancy and the subsequent abortion. Dana told me I would be well advised to steer clear of him. She didn't think much of him after her ordeal was over.

There was a pay phone in the hallway, a bathroom down the hall, and another roomer I soon befriended named John, a shy, sweet-faced boy from Windsor. John and I hit it off, I understand now, because we had both broken free of our working-class families and their aspirations for us in order to go to "The Big City" and become artists. I see now that my idea of becoming an artist was a much more romantic notion than John's. While I thought being an artist was a lifestyle, he knew it was a job. He set about the work immediately and didn't seem to mind having no money. I thought I needed a straight job to support myself while I went about the work of brushing up against artists in the hope that their genius would transform me. And there were lots of opportunities. It seemed everyone I met, except the Scottish Mods – young Scottish immigrants who wore Beatle-style haircuts and clothes and all held jobs as plumbers or carpenters – were artists of some sort. It was as if hippies were turning their lives into works of art. At the time I had not yet heard of conceptual art, performance art, or agitprop. My shy housemate from Windsor, on the other hand, had a real instinct for agitprop. Reluctant to share his $10 a week triple room with strangers, John devised a stinking and subversive method for keeping the room to himself. When he knew that management intended to show the room to a potential new tenant, he would place his jar collection on the window sill. The jars contained his daily urine output.

Although John and I shared a common class background, this was something that was never put into words. Perhaps we didn't have the words to express it, or it never occurred to us. Outwardly the frontier of hippie culture seemed wild and open and classless. Because everyone I met outside of work dressed in used clothes or inexpensive Indian cotton or blue jeans, the class origins usually signalled in dress styles were nicely, and conveniently for me, obscured. Evenings found me in the crowded comfort of coffee houses with hippies listening to folk singers like Ramblin' Jack Elliott and Tom Rush. Or I would make my way to the cavernous old Embassy Hotel on Belair Avenue to drink draft beer around small tables with the Scottish Mods, to whom I was immensely attracted because of their familiar accents and attitudes, tidy haircuts, and natty after-work suits.

I also made friends with a group of students who lived nearby in an old house on Huron Street on the block where the Robarts Library, scornfully known as Fort Book, now stands. They were from Etobicoke and had enrolled in the architecture school at the University of Toronto, although they didn't attend classes. Their home – what *Time* magazine would call a "hippie commune" – took my breath away and changed my ideas about interior decorating for ever more. You didn't need a couch and matching armchair from Simpsons-Sears in the living room with a coffee table in front of the couch and two matching end tables and lamps. The TV didn't have to sit in the middle of the room like a shrine. Nor did you need to hang a painting of a landscape over the couch and have school pictures and cardboard-framed snapshots on top of the TV with a big clock that chimed the Bells of St. Anne's on the hour.

You could have on your ceilings huge posters of French movie star Jean-Paul Belmondo with a Galois cigarette dangling from his lips, or a brooding Marlon Brando in a black leather jacket and T-shirt leaning into his motorcycle. Although the concept of private property was frowned upon, to discourage the stealing of food from unlocked cupboards in communal kitchens you could paste a picture of Raquel Welch on your cupboard doors, with a cut-out space for a padlock around the fly of her jeans. My student architect friends had spray-painted everything in their living room silver, including the single armchair and the telephone that sat on an orange crate. They had scrolled the words "Love, or what?" on one wall in three-foot-high Day-Glo pink, purple, and green script. The kitchen was furnished with assorted broken chairs, and the sink was full of dirty dishes. On the walls in the staircase leading up to the second floor, the occupants and the waves of visitors who trooped through the open doors had left their marks by scribbling life philosophies or favourite lines from songs and books. Bob Dylan was the most quoted, followed by Frank Zappa. On my way to the inner sanctums on the second floor I would learn that *"if God's on our side he'll stop the next war"* and *"brown shoes don't make it."*

Even in the mornings the stereo was cranked up full blast, filling the place with the sounds of Jimi Hendrix, Country Joe and the Fish, and The Velvet Underground. Joints were passed around at unusual hours and sandalwood incense burned in dusty little brass holders throughout the house to cover the aroma. Somehow it was thought that the incense would fool the drug police, who were always expected to raid. "Here, try this. No. It won't hurt you. Take a deep breath and hold it. That's right." The music would become louder and clearer and every word coming out of the speakers began to make perfect and profound sense. *"Feed your head... Feed your head."*

These people knew things I didn't about the war in Vietnam that was to kill almost two million people and turn more than a million innocent people into refugees. I didn't even know the difference between North and South Vietnam or that the war was just another face of the Cold War. Too afraid to ask stupid questions, I just listened to the men talk until I finally understood that – to these new friends of mine – the North Vietnamese were the good guys, connected with the Communists, and that their hero was Ho Chi Minh. The United States and Canada were supporting the South Vietnamese, the capitalists, the bad guys.

Although I had been raised to be an anti-Communist, I had a firm belief based on my Glasgow experience that war was wrong. I also learned that I could volunteer at an office on Spadina Avenue to help organize against the war and help the thousands of U.S. draft dodgers and deserters who were then moving to Canada. I volunteered at the makeshift office because it seemed like the right thing to do, although I don't think I did much besides answer phones and lick envelopes.

My new Toronto friends moved fast. To me they seemed to know where they were going, and they were always going somewhere. When they spoke they did so with tremendous authority, even if softly. They also looked each other in the eye when they spoke and had the bothersome habit of not laughing at my jokes. It seemed they didn't make jokes themselves, but enjoyed instead making ironic comments and sly observations about everything from architecture and fashion to the news headlines. "Did you see that ugly building going up at Yonge and Bloor?" "That guy in the polyester suit looks real cool, doesn't he man?" They would exchange knowing looks, snort, and gaze off into the smoke in the room. I would think a response was required and search around in my brain to find some appropriate reply. Of course no response was required or forthcoming, and I always ended up feeling useless. Where I had come from, smiling was considered a sign of respect. Here it was frowned upon. One guy named Mike told me I looked ugly when I smiled, so I stopped smiling.

By observing the customs of my new acquaintances I managed to develop a cool way of walking, and talking, and dressing. I read cool magazines and went to the foreign and otherwise arty movies at Cinema Lumière on College Street near Spadina. I remember sitting through hours of an Andy Warhol movie in which nothing happened and pretending to like it. It went right over my head. Same with a Jean-Luc Godard film called *Weekend*. I was scared to death by Ingmar Bergman's film *The Seventh Seal*, but again I feigned deep interest. It was easy to do because, as a woman, simple generic buzzwords were all that were required. "Right," implying concurrence, was good. "Far out," suggesting enthusiasm, was good, too. "You're not kidding," another variation on concurrence, was also useful. But the best of all the generic responses was "That was *fantastic*." It was the London Fog trench coat of language, versatile enough for use in any conversational weather. A bit of body language like rolling my eyes heavenwards also came in handy.

Gradually I had to fold up all my natural reactions and curiosity and put them away like a prom dress I never got to wear. In those days women were supposed to be *"obscene and not heard,"* as the writing on the wall also said: a whimsical John Lennon musing, from his book *A Spaniard in the Works.*

When I moved out of my summer residence at Campus Co-op it was into a second-storey flat on Huron Street, which I shared with my friends from Petawawa, Pat and Eileen, who had also made their way to Toronto. During this time I tumbled into unrequited love with "Steve with the Long Hair." Steve had an LSD-induced angelic face and played guitar on the flowering sidewalks of Yorkville Avenue. I would watch the clock on the wall of my cavernous Canada Life office, bursting for evening when I could head to Yorkville to find him. When he noticed me, he would look up from his guitar and shrug his otherworldly greeting. Then he would play again. I would sit on steps in a nearby doorway and wait until he was ready to come home with me, at two or three in the morning. Then I would make him something to eat and try to make conversation. The fact that he was not all there didn't matter. His lovely lean body, his golden hair, his serenity, were good enough for me. The fact that he never had any money didn't bother me either. Because of the work ethic I never managed to shake, I always had a few dollars in my wallet and I was always willing to share.

Besides feeding him, I paid the rent and bought records he liked, books he wanted, and tickets to events like a Donovan concert at Varsity Stadium, *"wearing my love like heaven."* It was so unusual for him to give me anything in return that when he presented me with a little book called *Gitanjali,* by the Bengali poet Rabindranath Tagore, I treasured it. I poured over it, believing that the words of the poet were Steve's words to me. After a couple of hours' sleep, I carried the leather-bound book off to work. It was my sign that, although I might look like all the other office girls, I didn't read *New York Times* best-selling paperbacks or Harlequin Romances (any more!) at lunchtime. In a nearby park I would lie in the sun, my sandwich and milk carton beside me on the grass, and study the poems until I could recite them by heart.

"*I came out alone on my way to my tryst. / But who is this that follows me in the silent dark? / I move aside to avoid his presence but I escape him not. / He makes the dust rise from the earth with his swagger; / he adds his loud voice to every word that I utter. / He is my own little self, my Lord, he knows no shame; / but I am ashamed to come to thy door in his company.*"

My roommates also had boyfriends who stayed at our flat, so it became a busy spot, something that did not escape the attention of our landlord, who did not understand that kind of hospitality, much less the current concept of free love. One morning when he came to collect the rent cheque he took a quick tour through the by-then artfully decorated rooms, bumping into our guests as he moved from room to room. "The only difference between you girls and prostitutes," he said, "is that prostitutes get paid."

We all laughed when he left. But I have not forgotten that thin laughter or the phone calls my father would make to me every Sunday morning to make sure I was up in time for mass. I never argued with him. There was no use telling him that I didn't believe in God any more.

Fed up with my monotonous job, I was soon riding the CN Supercontinental for Vancouver with a new love, a worker with the Company of Young Canadians who had a place for me to stay and some neat beaches to show me at the other end of the country. By then I had also tired of Steve with the Long Hair, who had taken to wearing a little shiny sticker on his forehead, a sign to the Venusians that he was one of the love people and that they could take him back to Venus with them anytime they saw fit. This new guy, unlike Steve, had a political conscience and was into community organizing.

Jobs were not as plentiful for young people in Vancouver at the time, so I launched what was to be a short-lived career as an entrepreneur. I rejigged Simplicity patterns to design and make medieval-looking dresses on a rented sewing machine and sold them from a corner in a head shop near Stanley Park. When my rented sewing machine was stolen and things got tough, I tried panhandling for the first time and wrote long letters back home telling my parents how it was possible to live without any money and still be happy. It was the only way to be free. By the time I awoke from the purple haze of my hippie years and moved back east, I had found something new to blame for everything that was wrong with the world. It had a deliciously vague, yet all-encompassing, name. It was "the system."

6

The Late, Great Sixties

In seeking our re-vision, thousands and thousands of us wan-
dered very far from "home," from our families, our communi-
ties, the values with which we were bred, the ideals with which
we were entrusted, the country we were to inherit. Along the way
we experienced corruption, disillusionment, pain and death, as
well as joy, but these were tracks to another "home," lives of our
own construction. This is true for every generation, of course;
what is special about having grown up in the Sixties is how close
our learning came to being revolutionary. You can't get much
luckier than that.

Myrna Kostash, *Long Way from Home:*
The Story of the Sixties Generation in Canada (1980)

IN SOME WAYS I missed the early part of the time that Myrna Kostash so lovingly and rightly celebrates in her book *Long Way from Home*. Had I been born a decade earlier, and had I not been working-class, immigrant, and female, I might have been active in the early sixties, in the peace movement or on one of the university campuses that she writes about.

I became politically conscious in the late, great sixties, just in time to join the cultural revolution at its midpoint. As the daughter of a recent immigrant I can say, however, that I didn't need the cultural revolution to learn what it meant to be a long way from home. When the time came, my jump into the youth culture meant only that I would move even further away from the community and the values steeped into me. I would abandon my immediate family, just as my parents had been forced – by the other political circumstances, of war and unemployment, to abandon theirs. We all paid a price, and I suppose we all gained something in the bargain.

Although I had been in the process of becoming a woman for a good few years, it wasn't until I returned from Vancouver that I began to understand how second-rated my position – the position of a woman – was. When I first entered what I will call my innocent womanhood, those of us without rich fathers and cars were being told we could attract men by flashing smiles and flaunting good figures. Okay, it was the same for women with rich fathers too. In the world according to *Seventeen* magazine, those not blessed with magic measurements or pert noses could work at developing their personalities and honing their intellectual or athletic abilities.

It had not yet occurred to me that the concentrated task of attracting men might not be an honourable life goal. After making a ruthless assessment of my own young self, I decided that I had neither the figure nor the personality. I was not agile enough to play sports as a way of meeting guys. On the plus side, thanks to my mother, I was a good housekeeper. I could make beds, do laundry, iron men's shirts, shop for groceries, vacuum, dust, knit, crochet, and put a basic meal on the table. At the time I could still darn a hole in a sock, if needed. I don't do that any more, but I do still like the smell of Pine Sol and the look of a spotless kitchen floor, and I have a fondness for the memory of white frozen sheets cracking on a clothesline. Thanks to my upbringing in general, I was a hard worker. But neither housework nor hard work carried much weight in the circles I was travelling in through the late sixties.

Unbeknownst to me, in large parts of North America, Britain, and Western Europe a cultural revolution was brewing, and this revolution would, in effect, downgrade all my nicely acquired feminine skills. In some circles the wife, the "struggle and strife" – a phrase my father sometimes applied to my mother – was going out of fashion as many women started blaming not just "the system" for all life's ills, but also, more specifically, the "patriarchal system" and the "male chauvinists" who ran the show. This revolution didn't happen in a vacuum, but was a direct result of the politics of war and industry that had reshaped the face of the globe after the Second World War. The Cold War world was not safe in the hands of men who put profit ahead of morality and peace.

But before I got my feet wet in sexual politics, I had to make a preliminary stop along the way in the still male-dominated world of student politics. I did this even before I was a student, through a job I got at the University of Toronto Library. It was there I found that certain left-wing men appreciated me. My God, they even had a name for people like me. I was what the father of the New Left, Karl Marx, called "working class." What my new boyfriends didn't know was that I was doing everything in my power to become middle class, like them. But if potential new suitors thought I represented the class that, along with peasants, comprised the politically chosen people, I wouldn't complain. I was easy. Sure, I would go for "overthrowing the state" and "grabbing control of the means of production." The trick, I was told, was to get the workers to act in their own class interests, break out of their alienation, and "rise up angry." It was easy to pick up the buzzwords.

Even as I said these things I had the sense that I was playing a part in a play that bore no relationship to my own experience of what it was to be working class. I could picture my father sleeping on the couch after work. He didn't seem to mind that he had few choices about where he worked, as long as he had a job. He didn't seem to mind that he had little control over the work he did and even less to say about who profited, except at contract time or during a strike. He had a deep and abiding faith, after all, in the nuclear-generated electricity he was helping to spread around the province. Or I would remember my mother climbing on the back of a snowmobile during a Kincardine winter storm – she would let nothing stop her from getting to the hospital where she worked, because she cared about her patients too much to let them down. Deep in my heart I knew I didn't want to be a cheerleader in a student-run revolution. I wanted an education, I wanted to be a student, and then I wanted a husband. And until children came along I wanted a good job. Despite my new urban experience in downtown Toronto and Vancouver I still yearned to live in a cute little suburban bungalow, the kind with the tidy lawns that my newly acquired friends had just fled. The slogan that feminist Gloria Steinem made famous, "A woman without a man is like a fish without a bicycle," had not yet gained common currency.

Because of the postwar baby boom, universities were bulging with young people in the late 1960s, helped out by the availability of student loans. My generation was crowded together in these places, getting to know each other and swapping ideas. The student radical culture was a heady meeting place of contradictions. The more privileged members could slip home on weekends, hold their noses, and partake in the lifestyles they condemned. They could even reject straight jobs, because in the back of their minds they knew they had inheritances or trust funds to look forward to. I didn't have that luxury. I was still working a job and only dreaming of going to university.

But the major contradiction in the student culture, funnily enough to me, was the ambivalence I encountered about higher education itself. One night a well-meaning new friend tried to talk me out of going to university. Although he was himself working towards a masters degree in law, he feared a "bourgeois" university education would spoil a working-class girl like me. We were sitting on the floor in a room about ten storeys above Bloor Street, in Rochdale College, when that smoky candlelight and wine conversation took place. He was bright and articulate, with a passion for his studies, particularly Native rights. He told me he was an anarchist. I only half-listened as he patiently explained his complicated political philosophy. I was noticing his lovely, long hair, which he wore parted in the centre. I was staring into his sparkling eyes behind the round, wire-rimmed glasses he wore. I thought he looked like John Lennon, and I fell head over heels in love with the idea of him.

Those days, with the mighty help of alcohol and marijuana, my conscience could be tamed enough to allow me the occasional one-night stand, but would not allow me to get too comfortable with steady premarital sex and "living in sin." After only a few weeks, and against my parents' wishes, the young man with the long hair and I decided to get married. The wedding would take place, we decided and announced, in six weeks in Toronto's Old City Hall.

My husband-to-be came from a loving, intellectual Jewish family. I had never met a Jew before, nor had I ever been in a large home like his uncle and aunt's place in Toronto's Lawrence and Dufferin neighbourhood, with their catered parties, maids who served food, and loud and noisy conversations about everything under the sun. I flew into a blind panic the week before I was to attend a party his aunt and uncle were throwing to celebrate our engagement. I was a nail-biter, and now I noticed the shape my hands were in. I rarely went to a hairdresser, and now I noticed my bedraggled locks and split ends. I had no decent dress to wear and owned only one pair of all-purpose shoes. Even though I had a little money to spend, I didn't know how to begin to make myself presentable. None of this bothered my husband-to-be. He was proud of me. I was a rose in his lapel, the very embodiment of his rebellion against his family's expectations. I was also a Catholic.

Like Eve must have done with her fig leaf, I managed to arrange myself just well enough to make an appearance. Not long after we got to the house I discovered, with horror, a run in my stocking, a difficult little problem to hide when you are wearing a micro-mini skirt. I had a glass of punch in one hand, so I tugged at the offending nylon ladder with my other hand until I had it positioned to run down the back of my leg. I glued myself to a wall and stayed there, nodding and smiling nervously until dinner was called. After it was over I was told by my fiancé (although we didn't use that formal word to describe our relationship) that next time I didn't have to help the maid clear the dishes, and I needn't bother blowing out the dining-room candles.

I have never forgotten the kindness of that family, and I really didn't appreciate then how far those broad-minded people had gone to welcome me. Only years later would I realize all the cultural rules we had broken by deciding to get married on such short notice. My own family was less broad-minded. My parents didn't attend our wedding, held in the city hall before a Justice of the Peace on a bright March day in 1969. At zero hour, however, my father did send roses and a card. My father's younger brother, Ronnie, represented my family – the same uncle whose first wedding had resulted in the family debacle that found me with the women and children locked in the kitchen while my drunk grandfather tried to beat down the door. Uncle Ronnie and his now common-law wife, the flamboyant and beautiful Bea, never let me down. Ronnie's first marriage had broken up, and his wife had moved back to Scotland with their four children. Because families keep secrets, I didn't know what happened or why, I just knew that Ronnie was now living with Bea and that Bea was from an "Indian" family living in Deep River. Bea had left her marriage to be with Ronnie in Toronto. Ronnie had started his own millwright business because he was "never happy working for anyone else."

At the wedding everyone arrived on time, except Uncle Ronnie. We waited. After about twenty minutes the wedding party heaved a collective sigh of relief when he rushed into the room. Ronnie told me later he had hurried from a job site in his work clothes and pulled into the municipal parking lot below the city hall, where he intended to change into his suit. After hiding behind the truck and removing his work pants he realized he had locked himself out. He smashed a side window with a tool he had in the back of the truck.

Years later I showed Ronnie a caption I had written for a photo-essay about my family. Ronnie and my father had served in the British merchant marine, both were millwrights by trade, and both had immigrated to

Canada. Ronnie followed my father by a year or two. The caption described my father as the conservative one of the two and likened Ronnie to a cowboy in a Buick, waving at girls and riding herd through life. My father had settled, sort of, into a job and family responsibilities. It was my interpretation that my father accepted life as it came. With a flourish my uncle grabbed the page from my hand and scribbled, "Ronnie, he just took it."

Neither Ronnie nor Bea was welcome in my mother's home. Besides believing that both of them had failed marriages, a mortal sin, my mother saw Bea above all else as an "Indian." Now, here I was, marrying a Jew, and not just any Jew, but a man shorter than me. I thought my mother would be pleased to have me marry a lawyer who was promising to show me the world, but she wasn't. Because I had no language yet to address these issues – racism and anti-Semitism – they just continued to run under the surface of our lives like a cold and murky current.

Given all the excitement of our wedding day, I don't remember making my vows. I don't think I really understood the seriousness of what I was doing. My husband and I, nonetheless, set up a minimal kind of house in a tenth-storey apartment at 70 Spadina Road. He studied at U. of T. law school and I worked as a library assistant at the Sigmund Samuel Library, saving our money for a planned move to England, where he had been accepted at the University of London. By fall we were living in a third-floor, one-room flat in London's Earl's Court district.

I landed a job as a placement officer at Brook Street Bureau of London, an upscale temporary employment centre. I worked from nine to five, and my husband's day at university started mid-afternoon and wound up late at night, so I was often asleep when he came home. On many fronts, my new husband was a progressive soul. He believed in student rights, worker rights, and Native rights. He liked rock 'n' roll, folk music, good food, and foreign movies. He saw the 1961 François Truffaut film *Jules et Jim* about a dozen times. It was a film about an independent-minded young woman loved by two men. He liked to travel, read, and engage in spirited political debates. But although he had opinions on everything and loved *Jules et Jim*, he had not yet absorbed the idea of women's rights. Then again, neither had I, though that was soon to change.

Occasionally in the evening he would invite me to join him at a pub, where I would meet his friends. Among them were Jane, who called herself a feminist, and Bob, a fellow law student. The conversation was usually about things I knew little about and was not much interested in, but I enjoyed the pub atmosphere and the excitement the group of them generated. Because I tended to be quiet, I think my husband often forgot I was there. But I was proud to watch him holding forth and, I guess, was content to be reflected in his glory.

I quickly discovered the joys of shopping on my own on Portobello Road on Saturday afternoons and the pleasures of strolling through Chelsea. Like my trendy co-workers at the Brook Street Bureau I began to favour Vidal Sassoon haircuts, Mary Quant clothes, and Boots make-up and cosmetics. One night while I was getting ready to go out, Jane came by and watched me applying my make-up: the lotion followed by the foundation, false eyelashes, the white line under my eyebrows, the green eyeshadow, and the drawn-on black eyeliner with "twiggys" – imitation eyelashes popularized by the anorexic British supermodel Twiggy. Then came the blusher on my cheeks and the lip-liner. Finally, the pink lipstick and a spray of perfume. I looked not bad.

Jane asked me if I did that every day.

"Sure," I said proudly. "I wouldn't be caught dead without my face."

My days at work weren't easy. Each morning I would arrive at the office to find a line-up of miniskirted and maxicoated "girls" – this was before eighteen- and nineteen-year-olds like me were called women – looking for secretarial or clerical work. With them were middle-aged East Indian men, with university credentials and accounting backgrounds, who were also unemployed. At that time Britain's human rights legislation prevented discrimination based on race. I learned, the hard way, that it was the job of agencies like ours to circumvent that legislation.

It was my responsibility to take down the particulars of each job seeker and make up a little card, arrange the cards in order, and keep them in a box on my desk. I had no trouble placing the Mary Stones, Margaret Macdonalds, Ellen McCaffreys, and Joan Palmers who could type fifty words a minute or had previous office experience. The men from Pakistan or India, or anyone for that matter who didn't have "British" experience (wasn't pure white of skin), were another matter. When I called personnel officers at the companies using our services I would give the particulars. "Age thirty-five, degree in accounting, sixty words a minute typing." Then the potential employer would say, "Jolly good, send him over for an interview. What's his name?" If I said anything that sounded foreign – especially a name I had to spell out – I would be told sheepishly that "The job . . . actually . . . had just been filled. Awfully sorry." Sometimes, even before I had a chance to describe a client's qualifications, an employer would tell me that he hoped I was not calling with any of those "jungle bunnies." The racism I had encountered previously had been silent. Here, for the first time, I could hear it, and it reverberated like a snare drum. It affected my sensibilities as well as my pay packet. I could get points only if I managed to place clients in jobs.

Soon my file was full of immigrants, people with families, desperate for work. No amount of persuasion or perseverance on my part made any difference. I felt powerless, but not as powerless, I'm sure, as the men I would find, each morning, waiting for me. They would show up at nine sharp, five days a week, in their good suits, their shoes shined, perfectly groomed, gracious and patient, holding their briefcases, newspapers under their arms, ready to work. And they would wait for hours while I made phone calls and tried everything I could think of to get them interviews – never mind jobs – that would bring them some hope. Since we spent so much time together I learned about their university training, I saw photos of their children and heard about their modest ambitions.

I tried to separate my personal feelings of affection for the clients from the work of doing my job. But soon I was having nightmares about these men in waiting. I began to resent it when a new face would show up and I was required to open a file for him. It was a classic case of what I later learned to be the "blame the victim" face of racism. At the time, I didn't understand. I got more and more depressed, and when I couldn't bear to go to work any more, I resigned.

At the beginning of that short-lived marriage I was happy and very much in love. During that first autumn together we went to Paris and then to Ibiza, Spain for a few weeks, and we enjoyed animated and passionate evenings in small cafés, drinking coffee or wine, until we couldn't keep our eyes open any longer. I loved French food, especially thin french fries. Because I couldn't speak French, and my husband could, I would eat, drink, and watch, just happy to be there in the world of the Impressionist painters and student activists. In Paris we stayed at a small hotel where we could have croissants, jam, and coffee in the room each morning. We spent many Paris mornings in a sunlit bed, chattering away and planning days of garden visits and gallery tours. When we visited the Louvre, I couldn't believe that the painting of the Mona Lisa was so small. But I tired of the tourist pace. The diet started to upset my stomach. I thought I was homesick. I began to make excuses to stay in the room while my husband went out alone for his days and nights of adventure. What was wrong with me? I should have been so happy!

It was during this time in Paris, between endless constipated hours in the small bathroom down the hall from our room and bouts of the blues, that I first read Betty Friedan's *The Feminine Mystique*. My husband's friend Jane had given the book to me. That book, as well as *Sexual Politics* by Kate Millett and *The Female Eunuch* by Germaine Greer, which I also read in Paris, changed my life by outlining the symptoms of "the problem with no name."

When we returned to Toronto in 1970 it began to dawn on me that, indeed, I might well be just as smart as any of my husband's friends. I was realizing that I had never questioned what I wanted, and somehow I had been led to believe that a husband was what I wanted. Now, regardless of what he thought, I decided I was going to go to university and get an education for myself. Because my high-school marks were not high enough to qualify me for university, I enrolled in two pre-university courses, in English literature and Canadian history, which I could do at night while still holding a full-time secretarial job at Campus Co-op. The history course was taught by a flamboyant young professor who encouraged us to call him by his first name, Steve. While I was able to keep up with the reading in social history I found I didn't have the skill to write the required essays, nor did I know history was a matter of opinion. I still believed it to be fact. So when I started to research the Winnipeg General Strike of 1919 I got confused when I read in one account that the strike was caused by workers' demands for the right to collective bargaining, better wages, and improved working conditions, and in another that the strike was more or less part of an international Bolshevik conspiracy, inspired by the Russian Revolution. I didn't realize I had to survey the literature, then make up my own mind based on the arguments presented. So I stitched all the arguments about the strike together in a crazy-quilt pattern and pronounced that the world was divided into two classes – the owners of the means of production and the exploited. I handed in the essay and anxiously awaited the results. When the essay I had laboured on and fretted over for weeks was returned to me I saw that it was marked with a failing grade and contained some cursory notes from the professor – but it is the comment scrawled across the top of the first page in inch-high letters I remember most: "purple prose." I had to ask my husband what it meant. "Empty rhetoric," he said.

Although demoralized, I kept working and somehow completed the courses, achieving passing grades that helped me qualify for entry to the new Scarborough campus of the University of Toronto the following year. But the history course had also steered me towards one of the most important friendships of my life, with Laura Weintraub, the exceptional young wife of my professor Steve. At the time Laura was a sociology student and they lived on Bain Avenue in Riverdale in a second-storey flat. Near the end of the course Steve invited the class to their place for a party that unravelled and careened into a screaming match about political theory. I watched Laura observe the drunken debacle from a safe distance in her kitchen. Silently, somehow, she signalled her discomfort to me and we formed some kind of pact. Steve disappeared out of my life a couple of years later, but Laura and their son Jesse stayed.

◇

In May 1970 the world witnessed televised images of the shooting and killing of four students at Kent State University in Ohio by National Guardsmen during an anti-Vietnam War protest. In the same month, in Jackson, Mississippi, the site of considerable racial conflict in the 1960s, police killed two students in a dormitory in Jackson State College. On October 5 the political upheavals hit home when James Cross, the British trade commissioner in Montreal, was kidnapped by members of the Front de Libération du Québec. My husband and I listened in silence to the broadcast of the FLQ manifesto. I was glued to the news and relieved to hear, five days later, that the Quebec Minister of Justice was going to offer the kidnappers safe passage out of the country in return for the release of Cross. Then a second FLQ cell kidnapped and killed Pierre Laporte, the Quebec minister of labour and immigration. All hell broke loose.

On October 16 the federal government under Prime Minister Pierre Elliott Trudeau proclaimed a state of emergency and implemented the War Measures Act, which banned the FLQ, suspended civil liberties, and imposed martial law. People could be arrested and detained without charge. Over 450 innocent people were arrested in Quebec alone.

Although the centre of the action was in Quebec, it spread in waves throughout universities across the country. Many professors and student activists alike were appalled by the sweeping legislation and joined with their Quebec counterparts in condemning Trudeau's actions. My two professors told us to watch what we said. There was widespread fear that the RCMP would use the War Measures Act to arrest student radicals. In those tension-filled days I was scared that all our political posters and books would get us in trouble.

I knew little about Quebec, except that when my family lived in Petawawa my father liked to slip over to the Quebec side of the Ottawa River to a bar called the Chez Charles, where beer was served long into the night, after all the Ontario bars were closed. In Quebec my father and my Uncle Ronnie were known to get into drunken fights, which some other guy always started, and come home with black eyes and missing watches. Myself, I had been in Quebec only once, on my honeymoon when my husband and I stayed in a pretty turreted room in the old Château Frontenac Hotel in Quebec City. I remember the cold, a tour of the old city in a horse-drawn carriage, and eating tortière and drinking wine at a table for two in a cosy restaurant, before a blazing fire.

Within a short year and a half, the blues, which had started like the sounds of a distant saxophone in the background of my marriage, had amplified and taken over my entire being. I found myself thinking that the marriage was a mistake. Things that had charmed me not that long ago were now driving me crazy, like his habit of circling in the newspaper all the movies he wanted to see and concerts he wanted to attend. When we weren't going out somewhere he liked to have his friends over to our place, and they had nothing in common with my friends or with me. Our life was guided by his cultural schedule, his politics, and his circle, with no time allocated to mine. I liked to clean the house, cook, and go to work. I didn't like going out most every night.

The dangers of drifting apart escalated when I met Andy Taylor, a student at the Ontario College of Art. In the summer of 1971 Andy had a job working with the maintenance crew at Campus Co-op, and we instantly became friends. Occasionally on Friday afternoons he and I walked to Grossman's Tavern on Spadina Avenue for lukewarm beef knishes and gravy. He had a small studio in an old coach house at the back of a student co-op house on Madison Avenue, where he painted and sculpted as his "serious" art and made silk-screen posters for fun. One day he appeared at the office wearing a fedora. The hat, he explained in an offhand way, was to cover the bald spot on the back of his head – he had caught his long hair in the beaters of the mixer he used to prepare the silk-screen dyes for his T-shirts.

Andy was gentle, kind, and self-deprecating and not at all into heavy politics. He was like a holiday from the intense political life I had encountered with my husband and his friends, who seemed to be turning everything I experienced in life upside down. I couldn't even watch the news in peace. Everything I saw, they pointed out, was not what was really happening. The good guys on the news were the bad guys, and the bad guys were the good guys. Multinational corporations with their interlocking directorships were war machines. I had no doubt that they were correct, but it was getting to be too much for me, and Andy was charming relief. One day as we were crossing Cecil Street on our way to Grossman's the wind caught the brim of Andy's fedora. He ran after it as it tumbled and rolled down the sidewalk on Spadina Avenue. He was a man chasing a hat, and neither my husband nor his friends were there to tell me that it was a hat escaping a man.

When I remember that day with Andy, the man who would later become the father of my only child, I smile. Nothing bothered Andy. He didn't pose. He was as natural as they came, and he reminded me of how much I liked to laugh. Andy knew I was a budding feminist, and "women's libbers" were then fairly rare and a new topic of conversation and jokes. He showed me a series of women's liberation posters he had produced that depicted a little pigtailed girl in a frilly dress holding her bra in one hand and a rifle in the other.

I don't remember arguing with my husband. I just remember going out one day, late in the summer of 1971, to get the weekly groceries. That day I did the washing and ironed all his shirts. I cleaned and vacuumed the apartment, then left, locking the door behind me. Looking back now, I see that it was not a case of not loving my husband; it was a case of me not knowing myself. If I had found the courage or the language to argue with him, he would probably have supported me, but I didn't and he didn't and that was that. Soon after the separation we made peace, but we could never return to the marriage. When I presented myself to Andy as a free woman, he excused himself politely and ran to a washroom to throw up.

7

All the Right Moves

The idea of awakening, sometimes erotic but not exclusively, goes to the heart of the fairy tale's function. But Sleeping Beauty's angle of vision, when she opens her eyes, is different from the point of view of the prince.

Marina Warner, *From the Beast to the Blonde: On Fairy Tales and Their Tellers* (1994)

ROCHDALE COLLEGE, which opened its doors in 1969, was a high-rise, student-run, countercultural utopia. The college, at the corner of Huron and Bloor streets in Toronto, was just a short walk from Campus Co-op, where I worked as a secretary. Although Doberman guard dogs and narcotics agents were not yet at the door of the alternative university, they would be within five short years. At the time, though, the waiting lists were long and I couldn't get in. Just as well. I didn't trust the new Rochdale College; it was too weird for me. By 1971 I had experienced my fill of the hippies who seemed to be at the helm of the intellectual and cultural experiment. I didn't want to study science fiction and Zen meditation. I was not interested in magic mushrooms. I wanted a real university education, like the one my ex-husband had.

I was much more attracted to the down-to-earth political culture that was then sweeping North American campus life than I was to the strictly theoretical version that my ex-husband and his friends had exposed me to. Armchair Marxists were people who talked about ideas. Real Marxists were people who did things. To be fair, the fact that I became a full-time university student myself in 1971 was enough to make student politics real – and no longer the abstraction it had been when I was the working wife of a university student. The down-to-earth politics on campus had sprung from the U.S.-inspired "Ban the Bomb," civil rights, and antiwar movements. But by 1971 student politics had been Canadianized and personalized by the War Measures Act, the question of Quebec in Confederation, and a healthy dose of statistics on the U.S. ownership of Canadian industry.

It was worth every penny I borrowed – thank God for the student grants and loans that were available at the time – to get into the university stream, because I wanted desperately by then to learn new ways of seeing and to acquire new analytical tools. For a young woman from a working-class background there were worse things I could have done than follow the call and drift, as I did, towards the study of political economy, social history, women's studies, and philosophy. As an excited young new student activist I submerged myself in the waters of Marxist theory and practice. I enjoyed reading books like Karl Marx and Friedrich Engels's *The Communist Manifesto* and Engels's *The Condition of the Working Class in England in 1844*. I learned about scarcity and about how my ancestors had met their needs. In so doing, some of them created "surplus value," or more than they really needed. When there was not enough food, shelter, and clothing to go around, the small and clever group that had more than it needed figured out ways of controlling the supplies. By learning how to manipulate supply by controlling production, they realized they could call the shots on almost everything connected with life – government systems, laws, cultural forms, religion, sexuality, and values. They could set the rules. Thus they managed to create wealth for themselves, and they established all-important sources and systems of power.

Marx taught that as people's ability to control nature improved, some compassionate new rulers were able to envision freedom from scarcity and want. They saw that it was possible to use technology and economic organization to overcome scarcity. But as capitalists created the *possibility* of liberation, greed got in the way. Lovers of crime fiction know that good detectives always begin by searching for motives. In Marx's investigation of the crimes of capitalism, of the hunger, disease, and violence that festered in the folds of wealth, the prime motive proved to be the unbridled passion for profit, which in turn drove generations of capitalists to pass economic control into fewer and fewer hands.

The task of people who decide to engage in "class struggle" for the sake of human freedom and dignity is to transcend the profit motive as the engine of change. But, for me, the central brilliance in Marx's theories was that it was *people* who made things change; not God, as I had been taught to believe. I found in Marx a powerful excuse for my departure from religion. As I discovered my reason, various fragments of experience and intuition began to click into tidy formation, with the delicious and satisfying precision of ballbearings. I discovered how to read books, underline important sentences written by learned people, and quote them to good effect. I learned how to dress up my own half-formed ideas in water wings called footnotes, and get rewarded for my efforts with grades – albeit, for the most part, mediocre grades.

In this new immersion in academia, I decided my vocation would be to challenge power. Not to run and hide from power, in guilt and shame. Not to court it, with deference and lies. My work would be to flaunt my new and conscious commitment to changing the uncomfortable and inequitable status quo. Swimming, perhaps somewhat overconfidently, in the choppy sea of new ideas, the rebel in me finally found her best stroke.

I was so excited about the things I was learning that I didn't even notice that a respectful or nuanced concept of working-class culture, my culture, was missing from the classic Marxist picture. It didn't bother me that the Marxist interpreters with whom I was learning described the working class, my class, like anthropologists or scientists observing their subject through the wrong end of a laboratory microscope. It didn't faze me that they could reduce unique, living, breathing people into what they called "the masses." Not realizing that most Marxists were not working class like me, I began to function with a kind of double vision – my kaleidoscopic and colourful image of my own class and the one-dimensional, black and white image projected by intelligent outsiders.

The same double vision applied to my sense of myself in relationship to men. Jill Vickers, an academic who studied women in universities back then, challenged male instructors who claimed that female undergraduates were their own worst enemies. In an article published in 1976 Vickers wrote:

> The norms of female passivity and inarticulateness, especially with regard to such topics as politics which are generally considered part of the male preserve, often make female students less willing and able to compete in the academic context. They tend to defer too readily to the views of others and the student who produces a brilliantly written paper will often be reluctant to display her intellectual superiority in a more public way.
> The assumption that it is better to be bed-worthy than brain-worthy is clearly not erased by entrance to university.

In some ways I suppose I was like any one of the thousands of young women entering Canadian universities in the 1960s and 1970s. But I didn't realize that as a working-class woman I was engaged in anything particularly revolutionary. Thank God for my innocence, for I must have been quite a spectacle – trying to perfect a graceful butterfly stroke with the anchor of my class as well as my gender tied to my waist.

In her article Vickers attributed the increase in undergraduate enrolment in Canadian universities to female participation. But she noted that this increase had not included working-class women in any significant measure. The class and gender conflicts of the time were amplified in the university-based new left; but Sam Gindin, a labour economist, cautions against thinking of the 1960s in North America only in terms of student rebellion. In his book *The Canadian Autoworkers*, Gindin points out that workers in those days became militant, too. Most young people then were working for paycheques on assembly lines, in factories, or in offices. The neglected reality – which he calls "the other Sixties" – was the reality of workers. Although young workers were sometimes hostile to the student movement, according to Gindin they were also still influenced by its anti-establishment drive and vigour. "As workers they expressed their dissatisfaction with the status quo, not by dropping out or participating in political protests; rebellion found expression in their attitudes in the workplace."

In choosing the university path by refusing to follow my father into a job at the nuclear plant, I entered a kind of never-never land. Working-class people at university didn't have trade unions they could turn to for building an analysis or for organizing.

The scattered reflections of that time made more sense to me recently when I encountered the clever character Timoteo in Primo Levi's short story "The Mirror Maker." Timoteo is a young man who invents different kinds of mirrors. To him, ordinary mirrors obey only physical laws. They simply reflect, "as would a rigid, obsessed mind that claims to gather in itself the reality of the world – as though there were only one!" Timoteo's secret mirrors did more than that:

> Some were coloured, striated, milky glass: they reflected a world that was redder or greener than the real one, or multi-coloured, or with delicately shaded contours so that objects or persons seemed to agglomerate like clouds. Some were multiple, made of ingeniously angled thin plates or shards: these shattered the image, reduced it to a graceful, but undecipherable mosaic. A device which had cost Timoteo weeks of work, inverted the high and low, and right and left; whoever looked into it for the first time experienced intense dizziness, but if he persevered for a few hours, he ended up getting used to the

world upside down and then felt nauseous, confronted by a
world suddenly straightened out.

The white mansion of the new left, perched on the shores of the Marxist
sea, had many rooms, with many mirrors of the ordinary variety, some
decorated in a revamped version of Soviet realism, others favouring the
designs of China's Chairman Mao. Generally, unlike the crumbling man-
sions of the old left (which I was told "had a direct line to Moscow") and of
social democracy (which I was told was "wishy-washy"), the new left was
freshly painted and innocent, and it had thrown its doors open wide, offering community access to its political processes.

I had acquired a taste of participatory democracy from my Company
of Young Canadians friend in Vancouver a few years before, and it was
finally starting to make sense to me. But I needed a political floor plan,
because my comfort on the terrain of the sectarian left was minimal, to say
the least. It was one thing to discover that I appreciated the wine on its
tables. It was another thing to know the distinctions between the many
tastes and vintages. Decoding the strategies and tactics of Marxist interpreters was another giant step I would have to take. The trick would be to
find a place for someone like me.

In 1971, the summer before my second year at the University of Toronto,
I was invited to take that giant step with the chance of joining an informal
Marxist study group. I thought the group, made up of a dozen or so articulate men and women, would help me with my school work the following
year. I was absolutely flattered to be included. I was a novice. At our regular meetings the men would usually lead the discussions about issues
raised in the books we were reading. There was a good deal of serious
talk about strategies and tactics and the Viet Cong. Sometimes women
talked.

When I read Thomas W. Dunk's *It's a Working Man's Town: Male Working-Class Culture in Northwestern Ontario* (1991), I found myself wishing he had been in that study group with me. Here is a working-class academic who stuck with academia. Dunk says that when he began reading ethnography and other kinds of anthropological writing he was hit by the number of unstated and inaccurate assumptions about his class culture. "Like most of us I was not, and never will be, in any position to debate the facts presented in ethnographies of foreign cultures. I was not there; the writer was," he says with an honesty I can appreciate. "I did not feel part of the collective readership. I wondered just who the `us' was, never mind who the `them' might be."

Dunk confesses that his sense of "outsider" status was evident to him, "if only in a vague manner." He found that the culture of the majority of people he met at university, and especially those pursuing academic careers, was different from his. "I had, for reasons I am still not sure of, left behind my working class culture, but had not made the transition into the essentially bourgeois culture of the university," he says.

Near the end of the summer my entire Marxist study group headed to a retreat centre just north of Toronto for an intensive weekend of study. After we arrived I quickly made friends with one woman, finding we had much in common. She too was from a working-class immigrant family. She too had broken with family tradition to enrol in university and become involved in student politics. She was articulate, beautiful, and warm, and I was immensely relieved to have found such a soul-mate. Her name was Deirdre. Her soul was Irish.

But for me that retreat was more memorable for the sauna than the discussion. Bed-worthy, but not brain-worthy, right? The wooden building with the sauna sat on the bank of a pond not far from the big house we were staying in, and after a cheery dinner with much wine and conversation we all headed to the pond, stripped, and crowded into the sauna. I had never been in a sauna, and I had never taken off my clothes in public before, but the rest of the crowd seemed to be treating the experience as if it were something they did every day, so I hid my anxieties – even through a kind of weird group massage in which each of the participants applied his or her hands to the back of the person next to them, then, on cue, turned and did the same to the person on the other side. I didn't want to be a poor sport so I hung in and did my bit, until finally, with high spirits, the group headed out to the pond to cool off with a skinny dip. It was a dark, clear night, and I tried to do the near impossible by keeping my eyes on the stars and the stony footpath at the same time – anywhere but on my naked comrades. I hoped nobody was looking at me. After submerging in the cold, dark water, I relaxed for a moment, at least until I found myself thinking about my mother. What would she do if she saw me now? She'd kill me!

During the weekend a "leadership" identified itself and announced the formation of a revolutionary group. Without knowing how I had got into it, I was now a potential recruit for a brand new Trotskyist political "tendency." I didn't know much about Leon Trotsky, except that he was a Russian Revolutionary who had fallen out with Joseph Stalin, and Stalin had eventually ordered him murdered. As a new "Trotskyist sympathizer," I soon learned that Trotskyists perceived themselves to be the "vanguard of the revolution" – the stationary engineers, so to speak, who tended the generator of class struggle and kept it functioning.

The other group members – especially the men – appeared to take this mission extremely seriously and seemed to know everything there was to know about the world. They even had a name for these people – heavies. I learned to keep my mouth shut when the heavies were around. My desire for "nice things," for example, I kept to myself, because I knew I could be accused of having one of those "false consciousnesses," which meant that you didn't recognize your real class interests.

The concept of false consciousness became a core issue for me. Other Marxists concentrated on economic questions like surplus value, scarcity, control of the means of production, the relationship of the state to the individual, revolution, or the duplicity of social democracy. As much as I understood it, false consciousness meant that people didn't necessarily know what was in their own best interests; and this "not knowing" was a major obstacle to freedom.

False consciousness could mean that you might not know the difference between friends and enemies, between right and wrong. It meant you could actually love your oppressors. But it struck me that my Marxist contemporaries seemed more concerned about what my consciousness *ought to be* than with what it was. Surely if people didn't know their own interests, then a logical starting point would be to define what you thought your interests actually were, or should be, then to examine the pitfalls – if any – in your belief. For instance, I fully believed it was in my interests to make a marriage work. To my revolutionary friends, this was the wrong approach to life's activities. At one meeting, when I did manage to squeak out an observation like "maybe women are a class too," the idea was quickly dismissed and easily forgotten.

I liked most of these people. They threw great parties and they appreciated good food. They liked to sing and dance and make music. Some played in rock bands. They read poetry. They liked sex. New couples formed and disbanded almost weekly. It was not correct to be jealous and possessive, although everybody was. In all fairness, if I had not become overwhelmed by everything I believed I didn't know, I could have had a great time. Politics, as defined by Revolutionary Marxists, were far beyond my sphere of immediate interest, so no matter how often the theory of permanent revolution was explained to me, I couldn't get it. I had no place to put it in the files of my own experience. Permanent waves, yes: a lot of us were perming our hair at the time. Even men, wanting to look like Jimi Hendrix or Bob Dylan, were doing it. I knew that home perms were tricky in the hands of amateurs.

When I was reading Dunk's book I found a curious reference to Friedrich Engels, who apparently described the working class of his day as people who "could rarely read and far more rarely write; went regularly to church, never talked politics, never conspired, never thought, delighted in physical exercises, listened with inherited reverence when the Bible was read, and were, in their unquestioning humility, exceedingly well-disposed towards the `Superior' classes. But, intellectually, they were dead." The passage made me think of my young revolutionary friends, who, like Engels, professed to respect the working class. My university friends, unlike the working class they claimed to respect, did a lot of reading and writing. They attended political meetings regularly, with the passion of the most religious of fundamentalists. They preached politics and enjoyed conspiring, analyzing. They studied with reverence Isaac Deutscher's Trotksy trilogy or Trotsky's own writings in translation, much like my forefathers and mother had studied the Bible. And they were curiously ill-disposed towards their own middle class. While they seemed to fetishize the working class, I still got the impression that they wanted the working class to be just like them. They wanted the working class to "pull themselves up," to become more like the middle class. Curiously, even though they despised their own class, they wanted workers to follow them in that direction. They seemed to think of the working class as some kind of beached drowning victim, waiting for the political kiss of life. I think we all believed back then that the world of ideas could be classless and free if we only pushed matters hard enough.

Even though I suspected there were large holes in this line of thought, I didn't feel able to speak out about it. I still loved my student friends. Fortunately for me, they knew how to play. And like the child I was, I was still seeking, more than anything, friends to play with. We all delighted in dancing the night away to Rolling Stones songs like "Under My Thumb" and "Brown Sugar" – songs I later came to see had troublesome lyrics.

Engels's observations about the working class, excepting the part about physical exercise, were a fairly accurate description of my grandparents' lives, though the profile was not an exact fit. My grandparents were not intellectually dead, nor were my parents or my siblings. While they did not want to make a career out of intellectual work, as I did, my family knew the ground it stood on. To prove this, I made a point of frequently bringing friends home with me to Kincardine to meet my family.

While Robert and Janis may have been uninterested in many things that were important to the Toronto intellectuals, I was well aware of a certain cultural richness existing in our family. The working class, like any culture, has its own division of labour, and that includes manual, intellectual, and creative work. My guests, who didn't take the time to get to know Robert and Janis, did not grasp this. I always knew my siblings had tremendous common sense and were astute observers and social commentators in their own right. I never saw them as underdeveloped versions of some other social or class form. One guest was so knocked out by my mother's many bowling trophies and the velvet painting over the couch that he pulled out his camera and shot a roll of film slides of her living room when she wasn't home. What he saw through his lens as kitsch, my mother saw as accomplishment and beauty. Dunk, whom I wish could have been there, addresses this process in his book when he notes that popular or traditional beliefs and practices "are at best ignored and at worst treated with disdain; their relationship to political practices and ideologies is not viewed as a concern."

My brother and sister, like the people that Dunk discusses in his work, wrapped their observations in humour, proverbs, jokes, and anecdotes. Unlike the big theories and dogmas I was beginning to learn, my siblings' wisdom came in economical packages. It packed the same punch, although it was neither for nor against capitalism and was tempered by a sense of limits I was no longer willing to accept. For instance, when I was most full of myself and my new lives, I would preach to my sister Janis about my newly acquired theories around women's liberation. I would give her books and make suggestions about what she should be doing with her life. Janis would listen politely for a few minutes before her eyes would begin to glaze over. Then she would get up from the table and put on a CCR or Eric Clapton record. She might ask me a question, like "What's the difference between Kincardine girls and the garbage?" I would start to correct her language, reminding her that the word was "women," not "girls." But she would ignore me to deliver the punch line. "In Kincardine the garbage gets taken out at least once a week." She would dance by my chair and laugh, having informed me that she knew what I was talking about but I didn't need to use so many fancy words.

The acceptance of limits is something that drives many left-wing intellectuals mad. This is not to say that my brother and sister don't feel anger and frustration when slammed against the boards. But rage is only one emotion on a rich emotional spectrum. Like all things, rage has its place – when rights earned are threatened, for instance, or when jobs are taken away, or, of course, when people are drunk.

In the course of his research with working-class men, whom he calls respectfully "the Boys," Dunk notes, "Marxism as a formal political doctrine is a bourgeois intellectual product. As such it is not, and never will be, popular among people like the Boys, at least not in its academic formal version." He continues:

> Given their subordinate position in society, the Boys react by celebrating what they have – their own ideas about what counts as knowledge, their own ideas about which cultural practices are important. This does limit their ability to develop a full and systematic critique of the system, but it is wrong to argue that this results from a passive acceptance of other non-class discourses. The Boys actively resist their subordination by creating another system of meaning. In this sense, they are cultural "bricoleurs," creating a meaningful universe in which they are morally and intellectually dominant.

Student radicals, in contrast, took everything, including themselves, so seriously. Adopting an equally serious attitude was one of the things I learned at university, but it certainly didn't come easily. To eventually find a balance between the two postures of seriousness and lightheartedness, or humour, was even more difficult.

86

◇

A highlight of my short-lived experience as a Trotskyist sympathizer took place on a sunny day in June 1972.

Some comrades invited me to join them for a car ride to Orillia, Ontario, where we would attend a provincial council meeting of the NDP. My father, coming from a Labour Party background, had always voted NDP. In my high-school years in Pembroke I had supported the NDP candidate in a mock election because he was the best-looking candidate in the race. But that's about as much experience or knowledge as I had about the party of workers and farmers and "ordinary people." In the car I heard that the NDP council would be purging the Waffle, a group of more radical elements, from its ranks. We in the car, it seemed, supported the Waffle faction, which was militantly nationalist and socialist. The Waffle Manifesto called for Canadian economic independence and public ownership of large foreign-owned corporations. Neither of these things was possible, the Waffle believed, without socialism, and the NDP had to be pushed further to the left. I heard the names of Stephen Lewis and James Laxer for the first time. I was told that Lewis, the leader of the Ontario NDP, was the bad guy. He had capitalist leanings. Laxer, a university professor was, along with economist Mel Watkins, one of the Waffle's national leaders. What did I know?

In Orillia we parked the car and strolled to the site of the meeting. In no time at all we were back in the car, heading home. The purge of the Waffle from the NDP didn't take long. Pumped with righteous indignation, some fellow-passengers in the car discussed the next step. Maybe the Waffle could form a new and separate socialist party. Maybe we had to keep trying to radicalize the NDP from within, and the Waffle had made a big mistake in pushing too hard. Maybe we should avoid parliamentary politics and concentrate on organizing the workplace. I enjoyed the scenery; I enjoyed the company. It was a beautiful day. But I didn't think of myself as being a part of a history-making event. I was not part of it. I was a spectator.

I was open to these experiences – fraught as they were with questions and uncertainties – because I wanted so much to be part of that bourgeois culture – the "better life" – that I thought would make me a better person. Although the Marxism I encountered in the early 1970s was a male, middle-class, and white culture, it was attractive to me, perhaps for the simple reason that – other than in the working class itself – nowhere else was the working class given *any* recognition. Even if some lefties insisted on viewing the working class as a mass of downtrodden wretches who had to be rescued from their fate, stirred into action, Marxism would have a major impact on my thinking and behaviour for many years, and still does.

That is why I was a willing volunteer when many of my male professors, puffed like peacocks, tried to sharpen my mind and rope me into the political culture that made so much sense to them. One essay question assigned to me was something like "Is There a Marxist Ethic?" I went to work on it, reading all the books on the prof's reading list about the Marxian view of human nature as well as searching out some titles from some progressive Christian scholars I had come to know through friends. Still trying, I suppose, to link my formative Catholic belief system with my new ideas, I argued that – to me at least – there *was* a moral and ethical basis to Marxism. This was a deeply emotional question for me. The professor took the time to counter my argument in painstakingly small handwriting on every piece of white space he could find, between every line, on my double-spaced essay, and I got the message: I was wrong. There was no room for integrated thinking in this new land. Religion was the "opium of the people."

Despite my abject failure to convince my Marxist philosophy professor that Marxism could be morally and ethically based, or at least to put my argument in a form that was academically convincing – my reading, writing, and debating skills were, after all, rudimentary – I have, often secretly, held onto my belief ever since. I continue to appreciate Marx as a great philosopher. His rage against the evils he witnessed during the industrial revolution sent him in a world-shaking search for the meaning of life. I too believe that starvation, exploitation, greed, and the domination of one by another trample the human spirit.

These connections were probably brought most clearly home to me by George Grant, the social philosopher regarded as one of the most spiritual and influential Canadian thinkers. Philosophers before and around the time of Marx looked for meaning in what already *was*. What distinguished Marx from the rest of the pack was that he was more interested in the ability of people *to create* their own futures. What still enchants me about Grant's interpretation of Marxism as I read it now – as the Salvador Dali painting of the crucifixion in the Glasgow Gallery enchanted me when I was a young girl – is his interpretation of Marx's insight on incarnation.

Christianity teaches, through the doctrine of incarnation, that God is not "other" to man because he "became man." Grant says that Christianity never came to terms with the massive social consequences of its own central doctrine.

Based on my university experience of the early 1970s I will always be indebted to at least one professor, Christian Bay, because he actively encouraged me to think for myself. Bay, a most gentle man, tried to get me to write more precisely about what I knew. But we found that the language I spoke and the arguments I was trying to make could not easily find their way onto the pages of the papers I was writing. "Why can't you write the way you speak?" he would ask in exasperation after marking yet another C- on a paper about class and ideology or women and liberation. What made Christian so exceptional was that he listened to me and was interested in helping me develop my capacity to think for myself. He was not interested in making me think the way he did. He wanted me to learn how to express what he believed I already knew. The best teachers, at all levels of academia and in all learning settings, are workers of the spirit, not just workers of the mind.

I remember driving several years later to Christian's home with my son Grayson. As we passed a group of men with pickaxes working on the streetcar lines on St. Clair Avenue, I was talking to Grayson about Christian, describing him as an intellectual. When Grayson asked me what an intellectual was, I told him that they were the workers we pay to think about things for us, just like we pay labourers to make the streetcars run.

◇

My entry into Marxism was only one of the breakthroughs I made in my first year at university. The second, and much more spiritually fulfilling, was my entry into feminism. The two things happened simultaneously.

Before I came into full contact with the women's movement I had no confidence in my own ways of thinking. I wanted legitimacy in the honoured traditions of the Establishment – the male left establishment at least. But that didn't last long. The feminism that had tapped me on the shoulder in Paris, while I was reading Betty Freidan and Kate Millett, almost knocked me over that first year of university.

Our first banners said "Smash Monogamy" and "Free Abortion on Demand." I saw quickly that all the books, newspapers, and movies I had been reading and watching were dominated by male thinking and experience. Most of my teachers were men. Most of the new left leadership was male. When I started reading female sources in the new U. of T. women's studies course I enrolled in I saw that the entire history of women's lives and identity had been muffled, distorted, and silenced. I realized that most of my decisions until then had been to please men, as in the case of my friends or teachers, or to rebel against them, as I had done with my father and the priest. Whether in the pleasing of, or in the fighting with, men were central. Everything revolved around them like atoms orbiting a nucleus.

I was soon squeezing everything I had previously learned through a new sieve of feminist analysis, observing with great interest not just the lumps left in the sieve but what came out the other side. I discarded my 36-B bra and stopped shaving my legs. I tossed out the lipstick. There would be no more miniskirts, no more false eyelashes. I began to wear Kodiak work boots, blue jeans and T-shirts, and a green, canvas parka. I was in uniform.

My new women friends and I began to talk, holding forth in kitchens, classrooms, workshops, and bars, telling each other everything – giving ourselves, not men, the political and moral authority for analyzing the world. I was now, strangely, miraculously, moving along a path that seemed to make more complete sense. I was lucky, I guess. Had I gone to work at the nuclear plant I might never have had the time to focus on the world of ideas and spirit I was learning to love. Still, if I had taken the path my brother Robert and my sister Janis chose, I might now have a pension and some savings.

8

Pioneers of Hope

*I think people who live their lives merely to live them as pleas-
antly as possible, and to have kids who will live them as pleas-
antly as possible, that seems to me inadequate as a life purpose.
I think you have a larger responsibility. And the trouble is that
often you've got certain skills and you can't find a way to use
them. You're in a society where there's no place for you to use the
things you've got, in some way that makes any sense to you.
What the women's movement did for me was say, "Hey, you're
useful." You know, life without that would have been really
sterile.*

Pat Schulz, in *Worth Every Minute* (1987)

I GOT INVOLVED in the publishing business and the women's movement
by accident – one of those accidents that, when I look back on it, was not
an accident at all. I'm talking about those incidents of serendipity and
chance, opportunity and magic coincidence – when providence comes out
to play. When I enrolled in the first women's studies course offered at the
University of Toronto in 1971, I just happened to be in the right place at
the right time.

I probably heard about the course from Jane Wingate, the woman I
had met in England through my husband. Jane and Robin Endres, Kay

Armitage, Ceta Ramkhalawansingh, and Ruth McEwan were part of the first group of women to teach women's studies at the University of Toronto under the umbrella of the Department of Interdisciplinary Studies. For the most part women had long been regarded as passive and inarticulate beings, especially in the male domain of politics and academia. The vision of the new pioneers of hope during the second wave of the women's movement reached way beyond academic rights. Male undergraduates, women argued, didn't have to drop out of their studies because of pregnancy or family responsibilities. The university had to address women's sexuality and social roles as well, and should provide the necessary supports, such as day care.

I still carry an image of teacher Ruth McEwan in a snowmobile suit, with a motorcycle helmet at her feet, sitting in a chair knitting while facilitating the class discussion. The topic may have been about women's oppression in its historical perspective, or women in the family, in revolt, in the struggle for suffrage, or in North American literature. If the topic was women's work, we would have been exploring the links between economic growth and ideology. Whatever we were talking about, I'd never seen a teacher like Ruth before.

It would still be about five years before the appearance of Frances Wilson's essay warning women to keep an open mind when it came to political ideology; that we had to be careful about turning women's studies into forums for political ideas defined by men. "The proper in-depth study of female experience," Wilson later wrote, "may point to completely new forms of social and political organization." At the time, though, it seemed as though all of us had much to do. Some of the instructors were organizing a women's film festival, and others were involved in establishing a publishing house. When I heard that a promotional leaflet was needed for the festival, I offered to do one, and asked Andy to lend me his art supplies. When I found I wasn't happy with any of my own ideas, Andy agreed to help, and we produced the leaflet art together: a simple line-drawing of a portable movie screen with the films and filmmakers listed on the screen. When the women saw the leaflet they invited me to join what was to become The Canadian Women's Educational Press collective as a graphic artist. I didn't have the nerve to tell them that the design was not entirely my own – that a man had helped me – but, in the end, it didn't matter.

During the founding meetings of the publishing house, in the summer of 1972, we decided democratically that the entire operation would be run on a collective basis. When I say democratically, I mean it in the sense that it was as democratic as anything can be when some of the people seem to know exactly what they want to do, and others, like myself, are more or less novices. Avoiding what was seen as the male hierarchical model, the group decided there would be no boss and no workers, and therefore no need, for instance, for a specialized graphic artist. We would all share our skills and train each other to do the tasks that had to be done – typing, filing, keeping books, fundraising, manuscript and policy development, copy-editing, proofreading, typesetting, marketing and promotion, design and artwork, and finding office equipment. It seemed to me that the organization represented the opportunity of a lifetime, and it was at the Women's Press that I developed most of the skills I have used ever since to make a living.

Appropriately, we successfully applied for funding to a program called Opportunities for Youth, established in 1971 by the federal government to provide summer jobs for students. Our work was dedicated to publishing works "by, for, and about" Canadian women. Women occupied few positions of political and economic power. We didn't control newspapers, radio, television, the civil service, or the assembly of information in the universities. Where women did have any control, like in the home, their work was belittled. Having our own publishing house made absolute sense. As I look back on it now I see those years in the early 1970s as a time for argument, for debate, for dissecting, for preaching, for getting the blues. It was a time for going into therapy, with a woman therapist, of course. When I wasn't attending classes or plodding through the writing of essays, I was at the Women's Press getting paid minimum wage to do a job that I thought was of the utmost importance.

I remember some names: Janice Acton, Cathy Carol, Lynn Lang, Genevieve Lesley, Laurell Ritchie, Liz Martin, Bonnie McLachlan, Judy Skinner, and Sandra Foster. I picture some faces: Margot, quiet and lovely, who moved on to I don't know where; and a Julie, not quiet but equally lovely, who also moved on. I know I have missed some, and that names changed as women took back their "maiden" (father's) names or separated from their husbands, and that others like Deirdre Beckerman, Rosemary Donegan, Dinah Forbes, Charnie Guettel, Lori Rotenberg, Pat Schulz, and Mercedes Steedman joined later as collective staff members or authors, but suffice to say it was a formidable group of women, with amazing ideas, organizing, political, technical, and fundraising skills. We were all white, and English was our first language. Although we didn't discuss our class backgrounds, I think I was in the minority. Most were middle class. At first I assumed that everyone was heterosexual, but eventually a lesbian couple felt safe enough to "come out."

The first Women's Press offices were on the third floor of a converted mansion on the north side of Bloor Street near Huron, directly across from Rochdale College. The quarters were cramped and stiflingly hot in the summer. We equipped them with begged and borrowed filing cabinets, chairs, desks, and bookshelves. I took up smoking. Working without a boss was not easy for me. I had no experience of being equally responsible to a group in any policy, production, or administrative role. But I was not alone. It was a new experience for everyone. Tricky problems seemed to pop up every day, often revolving around questions of skill.

Although the group had established that there would be no bosses, natural leadership and challenges to that leadership emerged. On the negative side I noticed women with particular talents repressing themselves for the good of the collective. I saw talented women tackled or frustrated when they inadvertently took the lead in a debate or activity. A great deal of what was then called "consciousness-raising" took place. This was a type of group therapy with a political objective. Sometimes painful experiences, like rape or the more subtle forms of abuse like neglect, were revealed and probed in what were probably irresponsible and hurtful ways, even though the members meant well. The group was so committed to revealing common threads that its members tended, unconsciously, or artfully, to ignore cultural and class differences.

On the plus side, I had spent years learning how to separate my personal feelings from what I was told were political debates. To my relief, at the Women's Press I learned that for women the personal and the political were the same. I was delighted to be absolved from that embarrassing "intellectual deficiency." I was delighted to struggle with questions I had never before had the nerve to ask. Was it enough to be a man's wife? If women marry, should they take their husband's name or keep their father's? What about the hyphenated compromise? Was it better to live common-law? Was the Pill safe? Was it enough to be a mother? Are day-care centres good for children? Should mothers let boy children play with war toys? Answers collided, contradictions flourished, the analysis deepened, and nothing was simple anymore. We would start with hypotheses, run tests, and evaluate the results.

There was talk of marriage as a prison for women, and of non-monogamous or common-law relationships as preferable. If a woman's place was not in the home, but in the world, and if women had to be revolutionaries, did that mean that motherhood was a lesser vocation for women? Because it seemed more realistic to assume that most women would not be revolutionaries and would elect to have children, and because women had given birth for centuries without the use of dangerous painkillers manufactured by multinational corporations, wasn't natural childbirth the best, if not the only, way to go? If women belonged in the workforce, it followed that workplace day care was the best way to socialize and raise healthy children. Again, looking back, it seems that in these discussions I became as rigid as hell. (But maybe, at the time, that was a necessary strategy.)

The housewife versus worker debate was a major focus. Since their work in the home kept women apart from each other, it was difficult to figure out how to foster group consciousness among housewives. As aspiring Marxists we tried to draw parallels between the French peasants of the nineteenth-century, whom Marx analyzed in 1852 in *The Eighteenth Brumaire of Louis Bonaparte*, and women who are dependent on men in their homes. From this kind of talk, which might take place after our meetings over cold beer and Wiener schnitzel at the Blue Cellar Room on Bloor Street, we found ourselves debating the idea of wages for housework. Maybe that was the way to organize and dignify the work of house-bound women, those Betty Friedan had diagnosed a decade earlier as suffering from "the problem with no name."

We were excited about publishing Charnie Guettel's short essay, *Marxism and Feminism* (1974), which we figured would be a worthy contribution to the various takes on Marxism buzzing around the movement. And we also talked about our menstrual cycles, our lovers, our dreams, and each other, like any women.

The first book we published as the Canadian Women's Educational Press, *Women Unite! An Anthology of the Canadian Women's Movement* (1972), was a collection of essays covering the whole range of topics and issues we were facing. I was keen on Sarah Spinks's "Sugar and Spice," an article about sexual stereotyping. We did the typesetting for *Women Unite!* at Dumont Press Graphics, a production collective in Kitchener, Ontario. I remember one late night on a bus ride home from Kitchener, when I was sitting beside Liz Martin crying my eyes out, feeling ashamed. I had sweated in front of a keyboard all day and had not managed to produce one perfect paragraph of typeset copy. We were using an old technology that produced a perforated tape that was fed through a photographic process to produce the sheets of copy. Reeking of chemicals, the copy would be hung to dry, like laundry, then cut, waxed, and put into place on layout sheets. I couldn't read the perforated tapes, so my typos wouldn't show up until the sheets were hanging on the line to dry.

Despite the frustration and self-doubt of learning on the job (a common enough experience) with less than up-to-date technology – technology that budding book production people today, with an available array of computerized equipment, wouldn't have to cope with – the book did get produced, amazingly, stupendously, and largely because of a collective pooling of resources and expertise. None of us, individually, could have manufactured such a mysterious thing as a book, printed page after page as perfectly as possible between two soft covers. Together, pooling our efforts, we could do things that none of us alone could have done.

We also produced a promotional poster to go with the book. Liz Martin introduced a few of us to the mysteries of the silk-screen printing process at the Coach House Press, a countercultural literary publishing house on Huron Street. The poster was black with a red women's liberation symbol in the middle. Inside the circle on the symbol was a high-contrast photographic image of women with their fists raised.

In those early years of the Women's Press, a number of the members of the collective were also involved in other areas of political action. Some, like Laurell Ritchie and Lynn Lang, had already been involved in the formation of the National Action Committee on the Status of Women and in the nationalist politics that had intensified with the Waffle struggle in the NDP, and had undertaken activities in support of autonomous Canadian trade unions. Others were active in a range of male-dominated left-wing sectarian groups. Some were becoming active in lesbian politics, and others, like myself, were pursuing academic credentials or gathering publishing skills. All of these agendas, some complementary and some conflicting, influenced the day-to-day running of the operation; and we ended up raising the issues not just in policy debates but also in our bedrooms at night.

I wanted the press to publish feminist Harlequin-style political romances because I thought they would sell to millions of women. I thought ideology was important, but that we also had to find ways of making new ideas accessible to a wider audience of women. I knew my mother and my sister wouldn't read *Women Unite!* When I showed that book to my mother, along with the various short stories and poems I was writing, she gave me some advice that I took seriously. "You'll never be a writer until you can write like Catherine Cookson." When my idea didn't fly in the press collective, my feelings were hurt. We did publish a novel about a woman who set fire to her house, killing her abusive husband. We published Rita MacNeil's songbook, as well as essays on the history of women's work in Ontario, which members of the collective researched and wrote. But they still weren't the kind of books my mother and my sister would read.

Marlene Dixon, an academic in the early women's liberation movement, was already writing critiques of feminism, calling it a "bourgeois" idea. "Oppression of women has different results in different social classes," she said in her essay in *Mother Was Not a Person*, published in 1972 by Black Rose Books in Montreal. She called feminism, as the term was then used, "a Pandora's box of troubles" for middle-class women.

> The fact that there are so few women who are directly experiencing material deprivation, poverty, threats of genocide or enforced pauperization – that is, are not driven by conditions of objective exploitation and deep social oppression, makes it almost inevitable that the search for cultural and life-style changes is substituted for radical and revolutionary politics. The relative wealth and privilege of middle class people makes it possible for them to envision a good life within the system as it is, even to create such a life through counter-culture forms such as communal living, or adopting lesbianism as a way to simply short-cut sexual exploitation.

By the time *Marxism and Feminism* was published in 1974, the Women's Press had refined its positions considerably. Basically, they represented a woman-sponsored leap of intelligence and hope towards a new socialism.

With a new acuity, members argued, for instance, that since women accounted for over one-third of the workforce, and the majority of those women were working class, making up the clerical and service base of the Canadian economy in addition to participating in industry, and because for these women the contradiction of their two jobs as housewives and workers was extremely acute, the crucial demands for working women should be equal pay for equal work, an end to job discrimination, good free child care, and paid maternity leave. To struggle for these immediate needs most effectively, to locate the cause of women's oppression, and then to fight it successfully, women in the movement had to develop an adequate theory that would encompass and move even further towards a definition of women's liberation under socialism.

It was during the production of *Women at Work: Ontario 1850-1930* (1974), edited by Janice Acton, Penny Goldsmith, and Bonnie Shepard, that I left the collective to focus on my studies. I was taking a women's history course with Professor Jill Conway and had immersed myself in the Toronto dressmakers' strike of 1931 with a classmate, Zoya Stevenson. I scoured the National Archives in Ottawa, interviewed old women about the working conditions of their times, and poured over census data. Another Women's Press member, Mercedes Steedman, was also interested in the garment industry, and for a time we worked side by side in the archives, learning about women's historic work and struggles together. (In December 1997 I was pleased to hear Mercedes on CBC-Radio talking about her new book *Angels of the Workplace*, a study of women, unions, and the "construction of gender relations in the Canadian clothing industry" – the result of her work started years earlier.)

I was well into this research when the Waffle proposal for Canadian autonomy in the labour movement finally made sense to me. Conflicts between the International Ladies Garment Workers Union, based in New York, and its local Canadian leadership, which was more left-leaning, dictated the sad outcome of the strike of 1931. The shots were called by the

U.S. labour movement, which was much less progressive than its Canadian counterpart.

My interest in the topic was not only academic. My maternal grandmother, Margaret Corr, sewed in Glasgow's garment trade until almost the day she died. The family story has it that long after Granny's eyes could see properly, and long after her fingers were able to sew the delicate finishing stitches on garments, her co-workers helped her make her piecework quota. They covered for her, so that she didn't lose her job. Money was so short that Granny walked to work, rather than spend the pennies on bus fare. Uncovering the history of the hardworking and brave women who worked in Toronto's sweat shops in the 1930s gave me clues about the life my grandmother lived and brought me closer to her. The research also gave me a deeper respect for the role of unions in the lives of working women and men. Unions, I realized, had played a large role in my own family's experience – my hometown Glasgow was a union town, and in Canada my father, Robert, and Janis belonged to the CUPE 1000 local and my mother to a CUPE hospital local at the Kincardine Hospital.

I knew that most women, like my mother and my sister, were not likely to go into public face-to-face combat with the men in their lives. Although my mother always called men "overgrown schoolboys" and could put my father in his place with one cold look or tear a strip off him when he let her down, she always said she would "scratch the eyes out of anyone who hurt him." In my home, the personal and economic interdependencies were deep, sacred, and practical. Men were not the number-one enemy of working-class women. Men, women, and children were all exploited by the monied classes. If the many positive ideas being promoted by middle-class feminists were to have any standing in working-class homes, I concluded, the labour movement, with its historic commitment to equity, was the best vehicle on which to roll them in. It became clear to me that if working-class women wanted equality, they stood a better chance of gaining this by working alongside their brothers in the labour movement than by associating only with middle-class feminists and women's liberationists, well-intentioned as they were, who seemed to be so out of touch with the realities of working-class culture.

After much reworking, that dressmakers' strike paper appeared in the *Women at Work* collection. The facts are there, but the passion that fuelled it, the spirit of my grandmother, is invisible and must be coaxed from between the lines of the paper's dry prose. It was my first published article. In the book I officially changed my name from its short form "Cathie" to my full name "Catherine."

In that article, in concluding that the dressmakers' strike of 1931 was typical of women's strike experience – the result of extreme exploitation, fought over short-term goals, and underlining women's status as second-class workers and their inability to gain effective access to the trade union movement – I was also beginning to map out a political and personal direction for myself. Since women had come to occupy a larger and more permanent part of the labour force, were better educated, and had higher expectations and greater responsibilities, we were in a stronger position to defend ourselves as workers. I would look to the labour movement – the workers' movement – as the place I wanted to be, putting it above any academic or professional aspirations I might have harboured until then. As I wrote in that article:

> Women are now recognizing their position as valuable and
> essential workers. These new conditions provide the basis for
> women not only to effectively organize and defend themselves
> as workers, but also to challenge the whole conception of their
> place in society and ultimately, one hopes, the society itself
> which has relegated them to an inferior position.

Generally speaking, the Women's Press was a middle-class operation for middle-class women and for many years would serve mainly middle-class purposes. Still to be heard from were the voices of black, Native, and lesbian women. Not until the mid to late 1980s, for instance, did writers such as Dionne Brand and Maxine Tynes get the opportunity to publish in the feminist community in Toronto. The journal *Fireweed* played a big part in this development. Nonetheless, the Women's Press was a perfect vehicle for many of us; it helped to get us moving. By cultivating that fragile myth of sisterhood, the sisterhood of all women, we learned to appreciate each other, we acquired knowledge and skills, we produced books by, for, and about Canadian women, and we made lasting friends.

Mercedes Steedman was one. Bonnie McLachlan was another. Bonnie was the mother of two little boys, Christopher and Jeremy. She was then married to Doug, who worked at the CBC. They lived in a lovely and busy home on McMaster Avenue just off Avenue Road, north of Davenport, which she made available for meetings. Bonnie worked hard. She baked her own bread and made her own granola. She kept a garden and cared for her parents. She was also a spiritual person, a side of herself she kept private. More public was a giant poster hanging on a wall of the house. The poster, one of the home's few signs of politics, showed Marx, Lenin, and Chairman Mao, with a caption underneath: "Some people talk about the weather. We Don't." In stark contrast were a baby grand piano in the dining room and a number of articles and furnishings that looked like family heirlooms scattered about the house. Bonnie and Doug had become politicized as students, and by the time I met them they were both committed activists. In 1972 I found out I was pregnant, and when I told Bonnie about it she invited Andy and I to live with them, rent-free. We accepted the offer. Andy was still a student at the Ontario College of Art, and neither of us had much money. We were struggling to survive on student loans and minimum-wage jobs.

Months later, a few weeks before my due date, I remember having what's called "an anxiety dream." In the dream my mother was my midwife. I bore down, like she said. I took deep breaths. I inhaled. Exhaled. Easy does it. Push. Inhale. Exhale. Breathe deep. Push. When the labour was over my mother presented me with a kitten. I was horrified. My mother asked me, "What did you expect?" Andy and I had taken prenatal classes, so despite the dream I felt prepared for the experience of giving birth, and I was planning on doing it the natural way; but I was by no means prepared for the challenges that parenting would present during the women's cultural revolution.

Grayson was born on May 8, 1973, a beautiful boy with ten fingers, ten toes, and a perfect little round head. Seven and a half pounds. When I brought him home from the Toronto General Hospital, I found that Bonnie had filled the house with flowers. In the living room, beside the fireplace, she had placed and prepared for Grayson the antique cradle her boys had used. She greeted us with rousing piano music. Bonnie loved Debussy. And she understood the importance of marking important moments.

Grayson slept through the night, right from the start. He took my milk easily. He smiled. He peed on my face only once before Bonnie taught me the secret of changing boys' diapers. As a mother, I believed that my body and soul had finally done what it was designed to do. I was in awe of its power. "Courting" in the seats of the 1939 Plymouth Coupe with Martin Quinn at the Kincardine beach, or making love later in my life with Andy, was delightful, but completely different from the intense physical and emotional experiences of pregnancy, birth, and young motherhood. In the mornings I would nurse Grayson in the rocking chair in front of the window in Bonnie's living room. From there I could watch people hurry to work. The mailman. The delivery trucks. I could hear the school bell in the distance. Then the silence. The distant chatter and laughter of children stopped to let my baby sleep, after he'd had his fill and his small mouth released my nipple.

There is a lovely old Irish song called "The Patriot Game," about a teenage boy going off to fight for his country. I heard it played on the radio one morning when I was nursing. I looked down at Grayson and swore he would never be a soldier. It was the age of love and peace. The war in Vietnam was on everybody's mind. It made no sense for mothers to give birth to killing machines that could die in faraway lands. But it was only half a thought. The half I chose to ignore, was a question. Would I want to raise a child who was not willing to fight for his beliefs? I adjusted my nursing bra and buttoned my shirt. I wrapped the blanket around his warm, small body and carried him like the treasure he was to the cradle.

I put my question to Laura Weintraub one afternoon, while she held her baby Jessie on her lap and as I struggled to change Grayson's diaper on the living-room floor, mother's milk soaking the front of my T-shirt. Laura reassured me by reminding me that contradiction was the essence of life. "Relax," she said. "It doesn't have to be this *or* that. It can be this *and* that."

By this time my mother was baffled by the life I was leading, and a little cynical about it. But when she came to visit and meet her new grandson, she made it clear that she approved of Bonnie. Proudly holding Grayson, my hard-to-please mother commented that Bonnie suited the name she had been given. Indeed, Bonnie – intelligent, beautiful, generous, and loving – taught me a lot about pregnancy, childbirth, and being a mother.

Doug travelled a lot with his work, and Bonnie and her boys settled into a regular domestic routine with Andy, Grayson, and me. Then Bonnie's brother Richard moved in too, and our extended family got even larger. We all took responsibility for caring for the household's three children. Bonnie often got up in the middle of the night if she heard the baby cry, and during the day she would take him for bike rides with her, strapped to her chest in the Snuggle Bunny. Sometimes one of her children would wake with the baby – like the night Christopher stumbled half-asleep to find the corn syrup to sweeten Grayson's soother. In the morning we found Grayson sleeping contentedly, his eyes stuck closed with syrup.

I think it was the first peaceful family situation, countercultural as it was, that I had ever seen up close, and Bonnie's house became a model for me of what a home should be. At the same time, though, it was hard for me to accept all the generosity. Sometimes I resented it. Given my deepening class awareness, I could see that Bonnie and Doug were members of the "other" class.

I'm sure it was as much of a surprise to them as it was to me, however, when my resentment occasionally jumped out like a hostile jack-in-the box. One morning, for example, we were all preparing for a Christmas party. Everyone in the house had tasks to do, and although Andy had mumps he was pressed into light service polishing silver. He should have been in bed, but instead he was sitting at the kitchen table in his housecoat. I knew how ill he was and that his testicles were as big as the mandarin oranges in the bowl in front of him. He was polishing knives and forks and spoons and other unidentifiable pieces of silver. I flew into a rage. "Who were we? Slave labour?"

After a flare-up like that, I always felt guilty. I loved the family, the house, the garden, the music, the books, the conversation, the domestic routine, and the new friends and acquaintances who passed through. Most days it was a house of laughter and joy.

Early each morning, before anyone was awake, Bonnie would rise and make herself a cup of tea. She would then go to her study and close the door and read until she heard the rest of the house stirring. I believe those moments stolen in the wee hours of the morning were the only time she had to herself. The rest of her time was spent giving to others. In 1973 she was editing Charnie Guettel's book for the Women's Press. I wonder how this spiritual woman felt when she finished work on *Marxism and Feminism*. That slim book would become a classic of the Canadian Women's liberation movement. Later Bonnie went back to university to study classics, teach, and in due course write her own book on Greek poetry, *The Age of Grace*. Time would also take Charnie away from academics and back to her first love, music and songwriting. Charnie, who wrote simple, country-style love songs with lines like "So I supply the questions and all the answers too/ 'cause talkin' ain't easy for you," could also write:

> The theory we demand for struggle is and will be a product of
> science which can only be developed fully in a socialist society.
> But even in its present undeveloped stage, this science is one of

our most important weapons. There can be no isolated super-theory of women's liberation. The next thing on the agenda is a more developed Marxist psychology to analyze sexuality, socialization, and the myriad of aspects of development involved in our liberation. And since this requires scientific and medical advances of a kind not yet available to us, the questions have scarcely surfaced, let alone the answers.

When Bonnie's mother became ill and in need of care, she moved into the house on McMaster Avenue. Although I didn't want to leave, the house was now too crowded, and it seemed fair that Andy and I should find another place to live. In leaving Bonnie's home I left behind a spiritual compass that might have helped me through some of the dark nights that lay ahead. Like most of the women who volunteered as shock troops in the army of women's liberation, Bonnie too had dark nights ahead. Bonnie and I would walk down different paths, occupy different positions in the fight for women's equality, but as was to be the case with most of my "comrades," we would remember each other always, and as tenderly, as men have long treasured their war buddies.

Laura Sky was another war buddy. Bonnie introduced me to the fast-talking, clever, playful, and stylish filmmaker. At the time Laura was the Ontario Director of the National Film Board's Challenge for Change program. She was from working-class, English-speaking Montreal, where her grandmother had worked in needle trade sweatshops and had made lovely clothes for her. Laura dressed with a flare and sense of fashion, complete with jewellery and lipstick, going against the grain of the "uniform" then popular in the women's liberation movement. Some people in our circle of acquaintances mistakenly took her appearance as a sign that she was not a real fighter.

Laura, a single mother with a small son, Adam, was taking on mother-hood as well as the male film establishment at the National Film Board. Later, when we were neighbours at the Bain Avenue Co-op, Laura and I spent hours talking about men, ourselves, our children, and anything else that came into our minds. We learned from each other while we put meals on the table and washed dishes and listened to the latest Judy Collins or Kate and Anna McGarrigle records. One evening, while abstractly discussing Lenin's theory of imperialism and the effects of colonization on the colonized, we began to talk about how deeply women's spirits had been colonized by men for centuries. I began to think of women as a culture, and not a class.

When I completed university in 1973 with a general B.A., Laura hired me on contract to write a handbook to accompany two co-op housing films, and then to promote the films and book and the concept of not-for-profit housing across the country. It was essentially a community organizing job, and the work took me on the road. By that time Grayson was in the Sussex Daycare Centre at the University of Toronto, and Andy had left art college to work full time on co-op and non-profit housing projects as a community developer. There's no doubt Andy took the job and left his work as a sculptor because we needed the money. But his reasons for leaving the art world were ideological as well. He told me he was sick of making art objects that could be purchased only by rich people. Community organizing would be his new art form, and affordable homes would be the objects he would create. Andy assumed the primary role of keeping the home fires burning while I was away. Even though our work dovetailed, and we worked together on the housing handbook, I became more and more involved in my work and in women's culture.

Grayson was three in 1976, when I landed my first post-university full-time job, with the Association of Canadian Publishers. Making the jump from the concepts of neocolonialism and women's culture (outright sleeping with the enemy) to the concepts of American neocolonialism and Canadian culture (buying the enemies' ideas and values) was easy. Most books published in Canada were published in Ontario. Most of the Ontario publishing houses were foreign-owned or controlled, mostly by Americans. In 1970 the Ontario government had appointed a Royal Commission on Book Publishing to examine the economic, cultural, and social consequences of foreign ownership. At the ACP I was responsible for developing and producing public information materials for feisty publishers like The Women's Press, James Lorimer, Peter Martin and Associates, University of Toronto Press, House of Anansi, Coach House Press, and Black Rose Books. I also spent months planning and organizing a national publishing conference, held in fall 1976. A highlight was an address by the federal minister of culture, Francis Fox, who reassured publishers about the government's commitment to Canadian books.

When the conference and its long hours of preparations were over I expected to be tired, but I didn't expect the total exhaustion I experienced. At first I thought I was catching the flu, and I stayed home from work for a few days. When things didn't improve I went to see a doctor, who told me to drink plenty of liquids and stay in bed. I complied, but didn't get better. I went back to work and didn't last more than a couple of hours before I had to leave again. I tried another doctor, who also diagnosed the flu and thought I was becoming overwrought. She prescribed Valium to calm me down. Gradually, over a period of several weeks, I lost all my strength. My eyesight and motor skills deteriorated. My eyes couldn't focus, and I couldn't stand up. When Laura Sky dropped in one afternoon to check on me she took one look and called for an ambulance. I was rushed to Mount Sinai Hospital. Within a couple of days I was diagnosed as having viral meningoencephalitis – inflammation of the brain and the brain tissue. By then I was curled into a fetal position. Andy panicked, I think, and stayed away to look after Grayson. Laura Sky became my main support.

In the hospital I discovered that my former professor, Christian Bay, was in the room next to me, also suffering from a viral illness that had made it impossible for him to walk. His mind and his energy were not impaired, however, and he became a source of comfort to me during those terrifying days and nights. He distracted me with stories and ideas, trying to keep my psychedelic, circus-like mind focused. As my body became less and less active, my mind became sharper and sharper, making unusual but seemingly logical connections and seeing everything with the enhanced clarity of surrealism. Since my speech was not impaired, I could talk a mile a minute and was compelled to share my odd insights with anyone who would listen. Like a cocaine user, I felt like the centre of the world, and everything that was not a product of my turbo imagination faded away.

Christian and I made a strange pair, the distinguished Norwegian-born scholar and his former mediocre student. On the evening of November 15 Christian wheeled himself into my room and turned on the television so we could follow the results of the Quebec election. Though everyone around us was in shock and dismay, we cheered when we learned that René Lévesque had defeated Robert Bourassa's Liberal government. Lévesque's new Parti Québécois of separatists had promised a referendum on sovereignty and won seventy-one seats. It seemed like Trudeau's War Measures Act had backfired.

Later I learned that I was the only one of six to survive the strain of Victoria flu that targeted the brain that winter. Laura Sky saved my life. I should have been joyful to feel my health return, but I wasn't. Even though I had walked away from my parents and my siblings years before, and even though I had let my work overshadow my marriage, I was devastated by the way my family handled my illness. My parents and siblings didn't come from Kincardine to visit me in the Toronto hospital, and Andy didn't come often enough to convince me he still loved me. He said that his role was to care for Grayson and keep the home functioning as normally as possible during the crisis. My parents said later they didn't realize how serious the illness had been. Nevertheless, in my weakened physical condition, and in the aftermath of what I saw as a brush with mortality, I was filled with resentment. I was feeling vulnerable, alone, and unloved, and I slipped quickly into the debilitating grip of self-pity. People suffering from self-pity may be able to function, but they don't thrive.

When I left the security of the hospital, I couldn't readjust to my life at home. My illness and convalescence took about a year. Although I had no appetite for food, I had no trouble drinking can after can of Newcastle Brown Ale, which I called my "liquid potatoes." I lived on it for months, slipping in and out of a general malaise and trying to cope with the regular hangovers that came with the territory. Andy and Grayson tiptoed around me, fearful of upsetting me and sparking one of my outbursts. I had no interest in them, or in even pretending to keep our house in order anymore. I slept long hours. I thought my only problem was that I was not strong enough to return to work. I thought that once I could get back to work everything would be fine.

But the problems were much bigger than that. I didn't recognize the signs of serious depression and alcohol abuse. If anyone else did, they never mentioned it. And if anyone was talking about post-traumatic stress syndrome, an illness identified after veterans returned from Vietnam, I never heard about that either.

9

The Dark Night

Our deepest fear is not that we are inadequate. Our deepest fear
is that we are powerful beyond measure. It is our light, not our
darkness, that most frightens us. . . . As we are liberated from
our own fear, our presence automatically liberates others.

Nelson Mandela, inauguration speech (1994)

I LOST MY JOB at the Association of Canadian Publishers because of the
length of my illness. With no protection in place for staff suffering from a
long-term disability, the ACP hired someone else. When I was physically
well enough to return to work, I circled an ad in the paper for a writer. The
job, as it turned out, was for a promotional writer, and I became the pub-
licity manager at the relatively new, provincially run, Harbourfront
waterfront cultural centre in Toronto.

Harbourfront's general manager, Howard Cohen, helped turn Toronto's waterfront into a public cultural and recreation centre as well as a high-
rise gold mine for real-estate developers. The communications director,
Fiona McCall, an extraordinary teacher, became my mentor. As a publicist
I was part of an eleven-member department that included advertising and
public information staff. It was my job to get media coverage for the Harbourfront Art Gallery, the reading series, the film and music programs, the
craft studio, the dance theatre, and the various ethnic and community

events and festivals that ran seven days and nights a week. In part the job involved calling TV and radio producers and newspaper editors and befriending journalists, making sure they knew what was going on and hoping they would be interested enough to cover the events. I hated making these sales calls, but enjoyed working with the programmers and meeting the various artists and performers who visited Harbourfront stages and galleries.

One day, for instance, I was at the old Windsor Arms Hotel just off Bloor, trying to make small talk with the world-weary humorist Fran Lebowitz, mothering her into doing yet another radio talk show to promote the Toronto launch of her book *Metropolitan Life* as well as a Harbourfront reading. Another day I was in a taxi en route to a television station, making still more small talk with novelist John Irving, in town to promote the release of his new book, *The World According to Garp*. Yet another day I was in the art gallery, running behind the bedecked, bejewelled, and bewildering Australian gallery curator Anita Aarons with my notebook and pen (I wrote catalogue copy for exhibitions) while she described the significance of abstract paintings. Phrases like "linear materiality" and "spacial alienation" meant little to me, but I jotted them down. Somewhat impatiently, Anita tried to convert me to her love of modern art and its preoccupation with form and technique. Generally, I liked colour and texture, I appreciated size, but I was much more interested in works that spoke directly to me. This exercise was only bearable because of Anita's boisterous spirit and wit. She herself was a work of art, as far as I was concerned. The art gallery work was also bearable because every now and then I would see a piece of work that captivated me. I returned to one piece of representational sculpture time and time again. The sculpture, titled "The Academicians," consisted of a life-sized group of monk-like figures, hooded and robed, with heads bent. The silent figures stood in a tight circle, their medieval backs to the world.

Harbourfront had a commitment to "community-based" programming, which was tolerated as the poor cousin of the "real" arts programming. I also had the opportunity to promote events like a fundraising concert for the new feminist literary and cultural journal *Fireweed*. I met aspiring filmmaker and musician Lorraine Segato, who held a day job in the Harbourfront film programming department. Lorraine, in turn, introduced me to a rowdy bunch of feminist artists and musicians who frequented the Fly by Night, a lesbian bar in Toronto's lower east side. The Fly by Night was like any other bar – the music was good, the place was packed and smoky – but there was not a man anywhere. It was unbelievable to me that such a scene existed. Many of the women who frequented the bar had, like myself, escaped the intolerance of small towns for the relative freedom of Toronto. I was attracted to the environment and to some of the beautiful women I met there, and admired what I thought was sheer bravery on their part, but I can see now that I was afraid to seriously explore the question of my own sexual identity.

Intoxicated by my work and the hectic life surrounding it, I decided I needed my own place to live. I am now appalled by the lightness with which I made the decision to break the marriage vows I had made such a short time before. When I talked to Andy about it, I presented it as a trial separation. In the many troubled years that followed I regularly accused myself of committing a heinous crime. Why did I think it was so necessary to leave Andy? Why was it so easy for me to convince myself that I didn't love him anymore? The shortcomings and problems of that marriage, the case I built to justify our separation, look flimsy and unfair from the place I stand today. Andy always was, and still is, a more than decent man, and time has proven him to be not only a good father to our son but also a loving and faithful friend. I loved Andy enough to marry him, and I love him still. I don't believe that "love which alters, when it alteration finds," is not true love. It is one kind of love, and it is as true and real as any. It would take me many more years before I would see that to be able to offer the devotion, loyalty, and constancy we associate with love, that I had offered so innocently when I made my marriage vows, I would first have to love myself.

My political analysis, by then fairly well developed in a Marxist direction, had not touched my soul. I had come to realize that for the most part the world didn't particularly respect working-class people like me and the other members of my family, but I had not yet rebounded from a lifetime of being looked down upon and treated as second-rate. I still took the insult personally. I also took it personally that I lived in a world that didn't respect immigrants without money in their pockets. And I also took it personally that I lived in a male-dominated world that restricted the role of and opportunities for women, of any class or culture. On top of that, I had moved from one country to another, from one town to another, from urban to rural, and then back to urban again. Dislocations like these had severed the continuity and balance provided, for example, by extended families. The extended family is one of the levelling ingredients in the common struggles between parents and their offspring. Enough studies show that the children of impoverished or otherwise physically and mentally exhausted families suffer most. I could never replace my Aunt Ada or Aunt Joan. We had working-class friends of the family, but no grandmothers to offer the comfort, the refuge, or even just the other ways of seeing things, that we had enjoyed in Scotland. Like plants, love needs root structure. It needs light, water, sun.

Chronic outsiders always have a struggle to fit in. Outsiders have to learn and relearn customs and security systems. They have to constantly define and explain themselves and get used to being misunderstood and misinterpreted. The problems of the chronic outsider are exacerbated, of course, for "difficult," or non-compliant souls like mine, and also by the size of the other changes taking place in the world. Some changes I was cheering for, like the women's cultural revolution; others I feared, like the ascendency of free-market capitalism. I could read toxic warnings in its stream.

Andy and I agreed to share custody of Grayson. Our son would stay with me for one week and go to his father's apartment the next. I was not the only one who had forgotten the wisdom of Solomon. I blush as I put this to paper, because I can't see myself making that decision now. Although I was opposed to child labour and supported quality, publicly funded day care, perhaps I overlooked broader and more nuanced notions of children's rights.

The guilt that stalked me after our separation interfered with that learning process for much too long. It was as if my will for freedom, inflamed by the ideals of women's liberation, had grown so large that it split the fragile moral skin in which it was encased. In pursuit of freedom I was severing my already insecure soul from the old and external moral codes, predicated as they were on women's subservience. In making that separation, however, I didn't think about replacing the old moral code with a new one. As far as I know this issue wasn't on the women's movement agenda, although Charnie Guettel had pointed to it when she had called, in 1974, for a more developed Marxist psychology. With the changes to traditional moral systems – rights, duties, mutual obligations, sin, virtue, sacrifice, conscience, rewards, penalties – came a loss of family support. I could find some solace and comfort from friends, as I had with Laura Sky, but something important had gone. In his book *Age of Extremes* Eric Hobsbawm says the losses of the twentieth century's great changes were more than material. "The compass needle no longer had North." My Catholic teachers would have called this phenomenon "the loss of the soul," although early Christians used to think that women had no souls. Life for me was like a film loop of a woman jumping from a flaming house. Over and over again, I hurled myself into the air. I was tumbling to the ground with no net below me. As Leonard Cohen sings in "The Sisters of Mercy," "It begins with your family, but soon it gets down to your soul."

I rented a room in a house on Hillcrest Avenue with a group of people I met through Deirdre Beckerman, who was Deirdre Gallagher by then. The men and women in the house were students or writers, and all were connected in some way or another to the diverse social, cultural, and political movements flourishing in Toronto around the universities.

None of them were parents, and once again none of them, as far as I know, were working class. When the Scottish poet and feminist Liz Lochead, in Canada on a cultural exchange, needed a place to live, I invited her to join us. Besides having set my heart on an eventual job in the labour movement, by then I also knew I wanted to be a writer. Liz and I had much in common. The two of us took the time to read each other's work, and Liz encouraged me to keep at it. She told me how long she had collected rejection slips from publishers before her work was recognized. Get used to rejection, she counselled me. Handling it is part of the writer's job.

The rest of us in the house glossed over our differences and made a lot of convenient assumptions in our attempt to run a communal household. They assumed I liked their casual housekeeping rituals; I assumed they loved to live with a child and share child-care responsibilities. The Hillcrest Avenue house was only a five-minute drive from Bonnie's house on McMaster Avenue, but it was a long way in terms of its sense of comfort, for me. The important thing for me was that the rent for the rambling place, full of character but in much need of paint and repair, was affordable when split five or six ways.

At that point I would have been smart to focus on my son and making a living, but instead I threw myself into another relationship. Adam Czerechowicz, whom I had met at the surrealistic house of students on Huron Street when I first moved to the city in 1968, had been the lover of my childhood friend Eileen from Petawawa. I had always liked him, and Eileen and Adam had been long separated by the time I ran into him again, so I had no qualms about embarking on my own relationship with him. In doing this I allowed myself to forget the many times I had held Eileen's hand as she cried in frustration over Adam. I knew Adam was not able to make a commitment to a long-term arrangement, that he was "not the marrying kind," but he fascinated and charmed me. He believed in sexual freedom. He loved women and wanted to be free to know as many as he could. In a way he was an entertainer, and his favourite audience was women. I enjoyed his performances so much I kidded myself that I wasn't the marrying kind either. Besides, by then I could even produce pretty sound arguments in defence of my decision to embark on such a bumpy ride. I was not being reckless (or so I thought). I was just busy trying to smash monogamy.

One good friend, Brian Williams, a collector of ware-ever pots and an amateur mathematician and philosopher, was fascinated at the time by left-brain, right-brain theories that were being applied to explain the differences between men and women. This dishevelled moralist, who lived in a basement at 50 Harbord Street amid his collection of pots, pans, and books, supplied the only voice of caution I remember hearing. A handsome and tender man whose love of language made him precise and clear, Brian predicted that "no good will come of this." But perhaps Adam and I deserved each other. We were excellent sparring partners. We made an art out of living outside of anything that looked normal. This was the man who had spray-painted the Huron Street house silver. He was also the painter who had turned an ordinary bathroom into the inside of a one-pint carton of Neapolitan ice cream – chocolate brown halfway up the walls, strawberry to the vanilla ceiling. When we weren't playing conceptual games, we were fighting and having fun. We liked music, art, reading, travelling together, camping, movies, taking photographs, cooking, entertaining friends, and staying up all night.

When the pressures of that relationship and loosey-goosey communal living started to wear on me, I found an affordable place of my own back at the Bain Co-op, near Andy again. Soon I talked Adam into moving in with me. Grayson remembers those turbulent years as happy ones. Rules were few. My reconstituted, hip family dressed in carefully selected clothes from Goodwill Services, went to movies together and to museums and art galleries. In the summer we took long car trips with music playing loudly on the car stereo – AC/DC and Black Sabbath for Grayson, The Stray Cats, Martha and the Muffins, Blondie, and The Ramones for Adam. Adam didn't like "whiny" women's music. I had to play my Linda Ronstadt and

McGarrigle sisters tapes when driving alone. "*Some say the heart is just like a wheel / when you bend it / you can't mend it.*"

It pleased me that Andy and Adam became friends and eventually decided to work together, which they did happily for years at a non-profit housing group, Lantana. Adam taught Grayson and me how to love the Bruce Peninsula. We spent glorious time in Lions Head, on the Chippewa Reserve, where Adam had friends, and exploring the nearby Graves caves, the location site for the film *Quest for Fire*. Adam had a lot more interest in Grayson's music and cheerfully taught him how to draw. For my part, I encouraged Grayson to write songs and poetry and tell jokes. We made a book of these, which Grayson aptly titled "Survival in the Woods." We spent magical nights on the Peninsula, curled in sleeping bags. I read George Orwell's essay "Why I Write," and Adam read Donald Barthelme in the tent to the light of a small bulb he rigged up to run from the lighter of the decrepit, gas-guzzling station wagon we drove.

Work was another world. When some of my colleagues (the programming assistants, secretaries, clerks, technicians, and groundskeepers) tried to organize a union at Harbourfront, management fought us with all its power. Since I did not have the power to hire and fire, even though my title was "manager," under the Ontario Labour Relations Act I was not a manager. I knew the union organizer, André Beckerman, who was then working for a small garment-industry-based international union. At one time André had been a representative with Local 1000 of CUPE, the power-workers union that my father belonged to in Kincardine. He was charismatic and persuasive and had a strong organizing campaign already underway when he contacted me at home one evening. After losing my job at the Association of Canadian Publishers because of illness, and because the Harbourfront pay was low and the hours long, I was more than eager to sign a union card. We tried to get as many cards signed as possible.

At the height of the organizing drive I was called into Howard Cohen's office and asked, kindly and politely, to explain my pro-union stance. While cordial, the meeting was in essence old-fashioned intimidation and scary as hell. I liked my job. I certainly couldn't afford to lose it. I even liked my bosses. But wages and rents are not psychological issues. As the campaign intensified, management hired a new receptionist to keep tabs on us. A management-friendly staff association sprang up overnight claiming we were all a big family at Harbourfront and didn't need a union.

In the end the organizing drive was defeated. Management used André's association with a garment-industry union to great advantage. Life on the job is not comfortable for ringleaders of failed union organizing campaigns, so I decided it was time for me to move on. Around the same time, Lew Gloin, the book editor at *The Toronto Star*, had been giving me the opportunity to read and review the women's literature that was flooding out from both left-wing and other marginal presses and mainstream publishing houses and was overflowing his desk at the tiny cultural command post he conducted from One Yonge Street. I enjoyed sifting through this material, much of which involved the unearthing of matriarchal societies and goddesses. But to me a lot of it seemed to be avoiding the key issues – economic inequity and all the associated racial and cultural secrets of that inequity. I understood the importance of excavating the past of female culture, discovering our lost histories and inventing new ways of saying things, and I made much use of the poetic and playful political possibilities that were opening up in this line of work. Now I see I was at the beginning of my search for my lost soul. In the left and through the women's movement, I had found the body. My next step would be to find the soul.

My cyclical urge to write fiction was emerging again. I was inspired by the life I was living and the hardworking writers like Daniel David Moses, Brian Flack, and Terry Kelly I had met through Greg Gatenby, the artistic director of the Harbourfront Reading Series. Gatenby was another person who encouraged me to write. He knew I loved the short stories of Alice Munro, for I had followed her work carefully since reading *Lives of Girls and Women* in 1971, when it appeared in paperback. Munro wrote stories about ordinary people living extraordinary lives in the countryside around Wingham, just down the road from Kincardine. She was a great cartographer of the moral landscape of the people I knew and the people I had left behind. "Ambition was what they were alarmed by, for to be too ambitious was to court failure and risk making a fool of oneself," Munro wrote. "The worst thing, I gathered, the worst thing that could happen in this life, was to have people laughing at you."

I still had some contacts in the publishing industry, through the Women's Press and the time I spent at the ACP. I was ready to try writing for a living. The decision was made for me during a dance performance by Montreal artist Margie Gillis. Not since the day I had gazed at the Salvador Dali painting of the crucifixion in the Glasgow Art Gallery had I been as moved as I was in the Harbourfront dance theatre when I saw Gillis interpret the Tom Waits song, "Tom Traubert's Blues." The soulful words spoke of confusion and despair. *"No one speaks English/and everything's broken."* Gillis was so fragile, the stage so large and cold. I was transfixed. She pushed herself through the limits of the music. She transcended the despair of the lyrics. I went out from the theatre lifted by the energy she passed to me. The next day I resigned from one of the best low-paying jobs I ever had, to try my hand at the lowest paying job of all, writing. Over the next four or five months I produced a half a dozen short stories and sent them out to magazines that not-so-promptly returned them to me with rejection letters attached. Waiting for the mail is part of a writer's job. But my time as a writer was shortlived. When the Women's Press, which I had helped establish, returned a story to me with a cursory rejection note attached, I was wounded beyond consolation, and despite Liz Lochead's earlier advice I panicked and lost all confidence in my writing.

I also panicked about money and started looking for freelance projects. For the next couple of years I patched together a series of such projects to earn my living. One was a research paper for the Canadian Council on the Status of Women for the International Year of the Disabled, a project undertaken with Laura Weintraub and Pat Schulz. Laura had worked in Ottawa for a time at a centre for people with disabilities. She tackled the issue of women with what we now call "developmental disabilities" but was then called "retardation." Pat, whom I had met as a student at U. of T. and who also had become a good friend, applied her experience to writing about the politics of cancer. I chose to research and write on women and mental illness.

I was still fighting depression and suffering from radical mood swings. My secret desire to form a solid relationship with a man and my equal, and public, desire to be free remained in conflict. My desire to be a good mother and my desire to be mothered myself, my desire to write and my fear of rejection and humiliation, were driving me nuts. My head told me not to accept what was considered to be "normal" behaviour for a woman in a world built by men, but my heart was at war with me. After surveying the literature and talking to a number of people, I came up with a fairly acceptable paper for the International Year of the Disabled book, and as a result I felt better about myself for a little while. But all the Marxist, feminist, and Freudian analysis I was doing couldn't make the pain go away. A note to myself in one of my journals of the times says, "the brighter my lights, the darker it gets."

What was wrong with me? Why did I take so many risks with my personal and professional life? Why couldn't I just settle down and behave? Why was I never satisfied? Would I ever grow up? I had some answers, but they weren't good enough. When I wrote the paper for the International Year of the Disabled book, self-esteem or spiritual issues were still outside my grasp. I was familiar with Marx's concepts of "alienation" and "false-consciousness." I knew a bit about the famous rift between Freud and Jung on the importance of sexuality in the cause of psychological problems. I also had a vague appreciation of what Jung was getting at with his focus on the individual's search for meaning in life – that mental health is characterized by unity in the personality.

I appreciated how he stressed the interaction between the conscious, personal unconscious, and collective unconscious systems. It was easy for me, a cultural Christian, trained in the Catholic school, to relate to him more than I could to Freud, whose obsession with sexuality only inflamed the special sense of guilt I carried.

It would not be until 1991 that I heard that feminist and activist Gloria Steinem was also struggling through those same years and almost broken by the same demons that stalked me. In her groundbreaking work *Revolution from Within*, Steinem observes that with the lack of what she calls "core self-esteem," no level of situational approval can completely fill the resulting emptiness inside – the "emotional black hole." The need for approval and community can become totalitarian. It gets so strong it can be exploited to make us work, compete, and serve in ways that clearly go against our true self-interests. "For the powerless and marginalized *this same totalitarianism means that no amount of self-destruction is enough.*" Feminist writer Naomi Wolfe was probably still a teenager when I started wrestling my demons, but by 1997, in *Promiscuities*, she had come up with a good name for at least one of them – "the Shadow Slut." The shadow slut stalked women who enjoyed, yearnèd for, and actively sought partners and happily experimented in their sexual lives, and it made them despise themselves for these tendencies. A positive concept of women's desire and sexuality remained unspoken except in the most clinical and political terms and was buried deeply in the women's movement for years. Fortunately, not far down my road, the pathway to self-esteem would begin to open to me, but I still had a few more mountains to cross.

Certain groups in the women's movement, those coming out of the left, were beginning to throw a rope bridge across the class divide. The group Organized Working Women had formed with the explicit aim of uniting feminism and trade unionism. When I think of oww I think of leaders like Pat Schulz's good-natured friend Lois Bedard and her sister Joyce Rosenthal, who have been present at almost every demonstration and rally I've ever attended and, I assume, at all the ones I've missed as well. The organization, still active today, has initiated many advances for working-class women. At the start, though, it was a war zone for women who belonged to competing left-wing organizations. The Communist

Party, the Marxist-Leninists, and the New Democrats were all vocally represented at its volatile founding convention. Laura Sky, who wanted to film the convention, was almost tossed out of the hall. As an employee of the NFB, she was denounced by someone as a state spy. The issue was resolved when Laura agreed to hand over the film at the end of the conference to the newly elected executive.

The boys in the labour movement, practical to the bone, responded to this challenge from oww and the left by establishing their own women's committee at the Ontario Federation of Labour and assigning the human rights staff person to handle women's issues. I was invited to do that job when the full-time staff person, Shelley Acheson, left on a six-month maternity leave. In those six months I had the privilege of working intensely with the OFL's first Women's Committee – with Julie Davis from the Canadian Union of Public Employees, Wendy Cuthbertson and Edith Johnston from the United Auto Workers, Deirdre Gallagher from the United Steelworkers of America, Frances Lankin from the Ontario Public Service Employees Union, and Lynn Vorster from the Communications and Electrical Workers of Canada. We were all working-class women, and feminists. Together, we designed and implemented a groundbreaking campaign for day care.

Pat Schulz was, by then, a leading spokesperson on the day-care issue. Coming out of the Trotskyist left, Pat had parted ways with her old comrades on that particular issue. She told me that the group she had belonged to – the League for Socialist Action – had decided to make abortion its main issue. Pat, a single mother with a young daughter, Katheryne, disagreed. She believed that a woman's right to control her own body was crucial, but to her a quality, accessible, and public child-care system that supported the economic freedom of women and children was equally important and needed to be higher on the agenda. Pat struck out on her own into the women's community with a mission. Being an intermittent single working mother, with Grayson in day care, I too had a personal stake in the day-care campaign.

The OFL sponsored hearings in communities across the province. Labour leaders sat on the panels and heard presentations from parents, child-care workers, early child-care educators, and social service providers. We held a province-wide conference, called Sharing the Caring, and organized day-care demonstrations at Queen's Park to bring the issue to the public realm. Out of that work came a policy paper, *Daycare: Deadline 1990*, which was followed up with a second publication, *Parental Rights and Daycare: A Bargaining Guide for Unions*.

I also worked on an antiracism campaign with the OFL. Labour had viewed racism for years as a force that split working-class people and threatened labour solidarity. Memories of the racism I encountered within my own family and in England, working at the employment agency and trying unsuccessfully to place the East Indian men in jobs, as well as the current television news broadcasts about race and poverty riots in Brixton, England, helped me get my head around some of the issues.

We produced antiracism leaflets, organized conferences, and prepared a high-quality TV public service announcement. Although we hired a racially representative group of actors to appear in the public service announcement, none of us around the creative table at the OFL thought about including people of colour in the conception and design of the campaign, or about hiring a production company from the black community to put it together.

At home the kitchen table was a busy place, where many of these issues and the political players met. Visitors praised Grayson's drawings and clapped when he demonstrated the breakdancing routines he was learning. But while I indulged him with toys and treats, my mind was often elsewhere, teetering on the window ledge of work, politics, family, and personal life. As publicly, politically, and intellectually productive as those years were, I can hardly bear to think about them now. On the romantic front, all I remember are the wild attempts to establish a monogamous relationship with Adam. We were the man and woman who, on the surface in my case at least, didn't believe in monogamous relationships. We had frequent jealous fights and quarrels over perceived betrayals, and rounds of constant drinking sometimes took the edge off the pain. My private life had turned into a constant party that didn't have the sense to end. I went to work dragging from lack of sleep, or hung over. I was consumed by self-reproach, but could tell no one that there was a gulf as wide as the Niagara Gorge between my public self and my private demons. My mother had always said, "You make your own bed and you sleep in it." That's what I was doing, and it felt like a bed of nails.

Although I was seeing a psychiatrist, I somehow managed to avoid addressing spiritual issues and my drinking at those sessions. I was a "poor victim of circumstances," more than skilled at putting a feminist or some other political spin on what was going on in my life. Men and the patriarchy were my problem. My women friends didn't understand me. My bosses were to blame. Or my parents and my impoverished childhood were the roots of my depression. Even when my doctor handed me a copy of the Alcoholics Anonymous *Big Blue Book*, I didn't get it. I gave the book to my uncle Ronnie. Alcohol had killed both my grandfathers and made life sometimes violent and unbearable in my childhood homes, but I didn't think it was my problem. I didn't make the connection, even though I knew that alcohol was a depressant as well as a short-term stimulant.

My depression didn't stop me from jumping into another new adventure, this time the world of film production with Lorraine Segato. It was Lorraine's idea to make a film about the life and ideas of Pat Schulz, who was by then dying from the cancer she had been fighting for ten years. With the assistance of the Women's Studio of the NFB, the Canadian Labour Congress, and the Labour Council of Metropolitan Toronto, we raised the money to start. Pat was a mentor, not just to me and the dozens of women she invited to her table for meals and conversation, but to hundreds of women who heard her speak at rallies and conferences and to the many community college students who knew her as an early childhood education teacher. She was tough and articulate on the outside but gentle, generous, and remarkably intuitive on the inside. The film would try to capture not only her complexity as a woman but also some of the history of the left and the women's movement. Of all the people who ate meals at my table and drank my wine, Pat was one of the few I remember who ever helped me care for Grayson.

When we were making the film I was forced to deal openly with the issue of same-sex relationships among women, an issue I had thought I could leave aside for others to deal with. Lorraine was a lesbian, and Pat was convinced that, although she personally could never go in that direction, the women's movement and the labour movement had a responsibility to support lesbian rights. I was not so sure about whether the labour movement, which was helping to fund the production, was ready to handle that issue. Pat and Lorraine insisted that it was me, not the labour movement, who was not ready. My own fear of lesbianism and the social stigma attached to being homosexual interfered with my ability to make the film that needed to be made. Homosexuality may be something that city people could handle, I told myself, but where I came from, it was still taboo. I lost the debate on the film and we agreed to include a section on lesbian rights. When I see the film today I am thankful I lost that round. *Worth Every Minute* was started in 1980 but not completed for years. Julie Davis, by then a recognized leader in the labour movement, introduced the film at its premiere in 1988 at the Mayworks Festival of the Arts and Working People in Toronto. Feminists like Julie were ready for it, but it seemed I was right that labour as a whole was not: labour education programs showed little interest in the film for several years.

Later, in 1993, I was pleased to hear that the Canadian Auto Workers included the film on the curriculum of the union's women's program. Pat and Lorraine had been so right to insist on giving language to women who have to address lesbianism, in their own lives, in the lives of their children, or at work. Even as she was dying, Pat took the lead – always ahead of the time and usually right. Pat wanted much more than to be equal to men in the world the way it was. "Men have a pretty crappy time of it too," she reminds us in the film.

Pat always stuck by me, although I was lurching from one personal crisis to another, when my drinking got worse. Others stuck by me too, although often they were either too polite to mention the problem or they didn't care about the mess I was in. But Bonnie McLachlan, Laura Weintraub, and Laura Sky drifted away. As for Grayson, I wanted, like every parent, to make my son's life better than mine had been, but the way things were going it began to look as though I wouldn't be able to deliver on that goal.

My mother had showed her love for us with the food she put on the table, the clean house she kept, and the clothes we had to wear. But she took little interest in our school work and usually missed the school plays or the open houses that other parents attended. In the earlier days, she was often tired after finishing her day's work as a chambermaid. When I was in high school she was a hospital worker doing different shifts, so her hours were out of sync with the school clock. My brother and sister and I were not encouraged to participate in after-school activities. We had chores to do, and then there was the television to watch. I would have to get straight home from school to peel the potatoes, make the beds, and look after my sister Janis. It was my job to vacuum – and to make sure I did under the beds as well as the parts of the floor you could see. "If a job's worth doing at all," my mother would say, "it's worth doing right." To this day I still hear myself reciting this mantra when I'm tackling my housework. From my mother's point of view, children learned from working in the home. If they were to sing, they would learn it from a mother or father. They would not go out for lessons that cost money. There was no time or energy to drive children to organized games or events, and there was no money anyway. Most extracurricular activities required expensive uniforms or equipment. Better to just go to school, do what the teacher said, get good marks, come home and do housework, then homework that neither parent could help much with, because they were too tired. And God help you if you got into trouble, because that too required energy, money, and time that was just not available.

But the things I learned from my working-class mother weren't helping me raise a child. I had moved myself into a middle-class culture in which work, politics, and play intermingled and divisions between personal and public life were blurred. I was openly affectionate with Grayson, and as he grew we developed a joking and bantering rapport. I didn't expect him to do household chores. Although he was bright and energetic he didn't enjoy the formal aspects of school. He made friends easily. I made only the necessary visits to his classrooms on parent-teacher nights. Like my own mother, I didn't pay enough attention to what was going on in his world away from home. But the house was clean, he had food to eat, the bills were paid, he had clothes to wear. On top of that, I encouraged him to think for himself, to read and to write. But he had so much competition for my attention. It was often easier for me to bring people home than to hire a babysitter and go out to meetings or public events. When Grayson brought his work to the table we might give it a cursory look and make some encouraging comments before returning to our own conversations. The friends might bring the beer or the wine, and I would do the cooking. Sometimes my visitors cooked. I figured Grayson was all right because he never complained about anything and seemed happy enough to be at a party every night of the week. Because Andy and I shared custody, by the end of my week with Grayson I was preparing his backpack for his move to his other home. On this kind of schedule it was hard to implement a regular routine or follow through on things. By the time he returned to my home, issues that had arisen during his stay with me the week prior would have been forgotten in our happy reunions. We always seemed to be starting over. So Grayson, though present and much loved, faded away into the growing static of what was becoming my barely manageable every day. Gradually I was what I swore I never wanted to be — an emotionally absent parent. In the battle between the public and the private, at that time the public was winning.

I gave up writing short stories and began to write poems, and I picked up a camera. Each of these activities took less time. I used the poetry and photography like therapy, and gradually found that putting things into words and pictures was a way of finding some meaning in my chaos. When I couldn't face reality, I could observe it quite comfortably from behind a lens. Adam gave me a Polaroid camera as a gift. It was an expensive habit, but the Polaroid allowed me to choose what I wanted to see, to focus on what I had chosen to look at, and to frame what I saw, the way I wanted it framed. By simply pushing a button I could freeze and capture my own version of reality. I have dozens of snaps taken at parties in the little house Adam and I eventually bought and renovated on Sparkhall Avenue, in Riverdale. But by the time we had ripped out the old plaster, removed the octopus furnace, and remodelled the kitchen and bathroom, I was in serious trouble.

That little camera, however, led me through many tough situations, including my amazing escape from the dead-end relationship with Adam. One morning – after a particularly nasty fight – I broke my favourite pink coffee mug on my turquoise tiled floor to make some point. Adam walked out, slamming the door in my face. In the awful silence I noticed a delightful contrast in the colours at my feet. I also finally admitted I couldn't handle a non-monogamous relationship. The idea of serial monogamy, of more than one sexual partner in a lifetime, I could cope with. I had already. But I was not willing to get good at polygamy, multiple sexual partners at the same time. I didn't like the consequences I had seen and experienced and I didn't like the lengths I had to go to numb myself in order to hang on to that idea.

I picked up the Polaroid and documented the state of my kitchen at that moment. I took pictures of the broken dishes on the floor, the pink and blue, the mess on the counter, and of Adam's professionally framed photographs hanging on our walls. I put on some music, showered, dressed, cleaned the house from top to bottom, went grocery shopping, and restocked the house with flowers. Feeling much better, I removed Adam's photographs from the wall, took them from the frames, and placed my own Polaroids of the morning kitchen in their place.

Then I made another photographic record of the new kitchen and promised myself that I would never again let my sexuality float on the open market of free love. I suppose this was a case of my own moral code, grounded in my own experience, finally emerging. The amazing thing to me was that it seemed a lot like what my mother had tried to teach me years before. Nobody ever listened carefully to wise women like my mother, especially not daughters like me.

Catherine (right) with model in the Vancouver boutique where she designed and made dresses for the hippie trade in the late '60s. [Author's collection]

Catherine at Canadian Women's Educational Press meeting, circa 1973. [Photo: E. Linklater-Wood]

Catherine at Toronto General Hospital, May 7, 1973, the night before Grayson was born.
[Photo: Andy Taylor]

Grayson (right) with friend Ramel. [Photo: Catherine Macleod]

Catherine with Grayson camping near Lion's Head, Ontario. [Photo: Adam Czerechowicz]

Family portrait on steps of Kincardine house on Mechanics Avenue. Top row: Mom, Dad, Uncle Ronnie. Front row: Bea, Catherine, Grayson peeking out, Aunt Jean, and Uncle John Macleod. [Photo: Adam Czerechowicz]

Robert at his home in Inverhuron with son Gregory, circa 1990.
[Photo: Catherine Macleod]

Janis with daughter Taryn, Kincardine beach, 1990. [Photo: Catherine Macleod]

Genevieve Leslie and Bonnie McLachlan at Canadian Women's Educational Press retreat in Richmond Hill, circa 1973. [Author's collection]

Mary Rowles, one of the "Ladies of the Immaculate Campaign" during OPSEU's Making it Public Campaign. [Photo: Catherine Macleod]

Artistic Director Maja Ardal and RWDSU Representative Donna Johanssen during Eaton's organizing campaign, 1985. [Photo: Catherine Macleod]

Pat Schulz. [Photo: courtesy of Katheryne Schulz]

Katheryne Schulz (left) with friends Tim and Samantha Edwards. [Photo: courtesy of Katheryne Schulz]

Laura Weintraub in backyard on Hampton Avenue, Toronto, circa 1982. [Photo: Catherine Macleod]

Katheryne Schulz at Garnock Avenue house in Toronto. [Photo: Catherine Macleod]

Artists' Union members at Parliament Hill in Ottawa, May 15, 1993. (L-R) Carole Condé with Mayworks poster, Susan Kennedy (PSAC), Scott Marsden, Cees Van Germerden, Clive Robertson, and Frances Leeming. [Photo: Annerie Van Germerden]

Eaton's organizing campaign rally, Scarborough Town Centre, 1985. [Author's collection]

(L-R) Carole Condé, Karl Beveridge, Don Bouzak, Catherine, Sharon Tobin, D'Arcy Martin, and Doug Tobin, at opening of CAW Family Education Centre, Port Elgin, Ontario, 1989. [Photo: Dave Hartman]

D'Arcy Martin, Catherine, Alex Clark, Tom Jackson, David Anderson, and Katie Pellizzari, at the Rivoli in Toronto during the first Mayworks Festival of the Arts and Working People, 1986. [Photo: Gayle Hurmuses]

Catherine and Bob Nickerson, first Secretary-Treasurer of the Canadian Auto Workers. [Photo: Dave Hartman]

10

Politics of Perception

I do not want art for a few, any more than education for a few,
or freedom for a few. . . . Art will make our streets as beautiful
as the wood, as elevating as mountainsides: it will be a plea-
sure and a rest . . . to come from the open country into a town;
every man's house will be fair and decent, soothing to his mind
and helpful to his work: all the works of man that we live
amongst and handle will be in harmony with nature, will be
reasonable and beautiful. . . . In no private dwelling will there
be any signs of waste, pomp or insolence, and every man will
have his share of the best.

William Morris, "The Lesser Arts" (1877)

LIZ LOCHEAD, THE POET who lived for a short while in the Hillcrest
Avenue house, has a poem about sorting through a house, fixing the things
that can be fixed, and throwing the rest away. "By hook or by crook," she
vows, she will get her house in order. Whatever it was going to take, I
swore I was going to pull my life together. I decided the first thing to do
was "get away from it all." In September I made arrangements for
Grayson to stay with Andy and took a holiday in Bogota and Cali, Colom-
bia, using it as a time to cool out and do some therapeutic thinking and
writing in my journal.

I returned three weeks later on a late flight into Toronto, looking for a fresh start. It was nearly two in the morning when I arrived at the airport in Toronto, and almost an hour after that before I got home. Once in the house I found that Adam had removed all his belongings – music, art, and books mostly. Because he had forgotten to close the front window I had to walk through a thick mess of fallen leaves in the living room. The place was cold. In the half-assed renovating job we had done, we hadn't replaced the furnace we had removed. I was facing winter and was going to have to learn to operate the small wood stove in the kitchen myself. Riverdale at the time was undergoing a massive renovation, with young professionals moving in and tearing the old houses apart. There were demolition bins in front of every third door in the area. Adam used to collect firewood for our stove from these bins. I was not about to assume that task. The leaves and the cold provided an inauspicious beginning to my new life. I would soon buy my first cord of wood and have it piled on the front porch for winter.

But that night, after walking from room to room, sizing up the extent of the changes, I decided to run a bath and get to bed. I started by sitting on the edge of the bath tub as it filled up with warm water and bubbles. I dragged my fingers through the water. I was not sure what lay ahead, but anything had to be better that what I had just been through. I turned the water off and walked into the bedroom and looked at the empty double bed. I threw my suitcase onto it, opened it up, and located a nightgown and toothbrush. When I returned to the bathroom I found I had locked myself out. Wearily, I leaned my back against the door and slid to the floor in tears. Finally, I called Uncle Ronnie in Scarborough. Within an hour he was sitting at the kitchen table with me and we were sharing a bottle of scotch he had brought with him for the emergency. I forgot about the bath and we drank together until the sun came up. When we knew the stores would be open we went out to buy groceries. There would be food in the house when Grayson arrived home from school that afternoon.

I had no trouble finding another job. A friend, Rosemary Donegan, told me that The Guild of Canadian Playwrights was looking for an executive director. The hours were regular, the pay wasn't great, but it was a stable organization and the pressure wasn't heavy. The Guild was an arts service body funded by the three levels of government that represented playwrights across Canada. When I joined the team they were working out the details on a minimum standard contract with theatre producers. Were not writers workers too – among the worst paid in the country? It seemed to me, sitting in that small office without a secretary and counting pennies before I made long-distance phone calls, that marginal groups of cultural workers like these should somehow build links with the labour movement. Resources could be shared and, at least, I would not have to worry about the cost of returning a call to Guild members who lived outside Toronto.

The Ontario Arts Council was a major funder of the Guild, and Walter Pitman, the former NDP MPP and MP for the Peterborough area, and president of Ryerson Polytechnic, was its president. In fall 1982, under Pitman's tenure, the OAC sent invitations to the Guild, the Writers' Union, and the League of Canadian Poets to join representatives of the labour movement at a Toronto conference on popular culture to be held at the Art Gallery of Ontario. Together with playwright Steven Bush, who with musician Allan Booth had just finished writing *Life on the Line*, a play about work, I went to represent the Guild of Canadian Playwrights. When speakers from Sweden described the inroads they had made in celebrating and funding popular culture, a penny dropped for me. I began to see the difference between "culture" and "art," two words I had always misused by interchanging them. Culture, according to Raymond Williams, is "a particular way of life, whether of a people, a period, a group, or humanity in general," and can take myriad forms: activities, relationships, processes. Art is only one form of cultural self-expression. The Swedes maintained that since all people are cultured, it's wrong that the arts of the ruling classes in all societies are allowed to dominate, so that expressions of popular or working-class culture get ignored. The work of artisans and craftspeople, for example, has traditionally not been considered as art. Unless stories exist on the printed page, they are not considered literature and not considered important. For example, working-class culture, like women's culture and Native culture, is generally an oral culture. The literature of all three cultures only passes from generation to generation through the mediation of talented storytellers, people like my father or my Aunt Bea. Yet storytelling is usually not called art.

Put another way, if you picture art – literature, films, music, paintings, or sculptures – as the mirror in which people can see themselves, people who come from families like mine – as I realized earlier – usually see nothing familiar when they look in that mirror. Unions and the lives of working people tend to be visible in the media only during strikes. And the trend in modern art has been away from representation and narrative, and obsessed by the abstract. In Canada, that's a big political problem because the arts are funded by taxpayers, the majority of them workers. In the early 1980s major public arts funding bodies, like the Canada Council and provincial arts councils, were funding only a certain kind of art, that of the dominant class.

The conference included writers and artists with few publishers and galleries available for their work and a few representatives from unions, bursting with stories to tell. Except for some professional media relations representatives, generally with journalism training, and overworked staffers who hate to write, there are few writers in the labour movement. It seemed to me, and probably to Walter Pitman as well when he designed the conference and extended the invitations, that it was time for the two to get together.

One of the speakers at the conference was Timothy Porteous, the head of the Canada Council, the national arts funding body. After we heard exciting presentations about the development of popular culture in Sweden through unions and other community-based groups, Porteous stood up and proceeded to argue that Canada had no popular culture. The whole point of the conference had gone right over his head. Since the Canada Council didn't fund popular culture at the time, Porteous couldn't believe it existed. Deirdre Gallagher of the United Steelworkers jumped to her feet and challenged him, making a brilliant impromptu speech about her own working-class roots and the rich Irish Catholic immigrant culture she had grown up in. She described the stained glass art she saw in churches as well as the song and storytelling she enjoyed at family gatherings and with workers at union socials across the country.

As Deirdre spoke I thought back to the theatres, first at my grandmother's when I was a child, and later in Canada in my parents' living room on Saturday nights, when friends gathered to entertain themselves with song and drink. Each performer was unique. Whether it was Mal Kears performing his version of "My Friend Sylvest" or Vi Graham singing "Danny Boy," each performer had a story to tell, and they told these stories to each other. You seldom saw their stories on movie screens, found their portraits in public galleries, or picked up a book about them.

Although the professional writers I was meeting through my Guild work were engaged in lively and wide-ranging discussions about Canadian identity and culture, they were struggling for audiences. Their work dealt with questions of national or regional heritage and – to a lesser degree – gender and sexuality. But for the most part they were talking to themselves. Like the publishers I had encountered at the ACP, and many of the non-mainstream artists I had met at Harbourfront, they were feeling irrelevant and hard done by. They were financially squeezed. Taxpayers didn't want to pay for art, and politicians knew it. This lack of support was not surprising: given the lack of recognition by the traditional arts community, most working people were suspicious, if not outright wary, of the arts. My family had almost laughed me out the door when I said I wanted to attend the Ontario College of Art when I finished high school.

After the Toronto conference a small group of us gathered around a table beside a mechanical bull at a bar on McCall Street. The main issue was, "What is to be done?" We discussed the points Deirdre had made and cheered her for challenging the head of the Canada Council. Karl Beveridge and Carole Condé, two artists who lived and worked together and often did projects with labour unions, talked about the ludicrous and inequitable division between mental and manual labour. Art, regarded as the embodiment of creativity, is privileged; most wage work, regarded as the embodiment of drudgery, is reviled. Maybe this was one of the reasons I had always aspired to the arts – as a way out of what I too regarded as the drudgery and boredom of my parents' work and my class; that I was somehow above the work of my own people and would have to jump class to be a writer. Karl and Carole made me start seeing that the working class had its own artists, and that working-class people should not have to abandon their own culture when they were creative with language and paintbrushes instead of lathes and hammers.

We talked about political connections too. The division of labour between mental and manual labour is a breeding ground for the dreaded, silent majority – at once the mainstay and nightmare of the powerful because of its unpredictable volatility. This division tries to reserve the sphere of ideas and creativity for its sanctioned published, exhibited, or otherwise commissioned/ hired minority. Language, images, codes, and symbols are class privileges. What is freedom of speech and democracy to people with no means of public expression?

Unlike most other areas of production, in the arts the revered customer of the free-market capitalists counted for nothing. Why? Because capitalism understands full well that the arts and culture – the Trojan horses of ideology – are its most powerful and most secret weapon. It is necessary, moreover, to keep that weapon out of the hands of the "enemy." So ordinary people are led to believe that they are too thick to appreciate or make real art. Though scorned for saying things like "I don't know much about art, but I know what I like," ordinary people are regarded as Philistines in the galleries of ideology, just as women were once thought of as having no place in universities, particularly in political science courses.

We had all heard the typical putdowns: "She has no class," or "he is so common," or "they are so vulgar," or that poetry is "too undisciplined," or "those paintings are so amateur" ("naive," however, if a market does emerge, as it did in the famous case of Grandma Moses) or "What's that little purple plasticine man doing in sculpture exhibition?" Sitting around that barroom table we began to develop strategies. Karl and Carole argued that the labour movement defended workers on the shop floor/office, improved working conditions, made life better for retirees, but what did it do about life *off* the job – more than half a worker's life – the leisure time, recreation time, and cultural time? The labour movement has to mobilize for alternative economics, against racism and sexism, for economically viable environmental policies, but how can labour do this work when its members are continually told by the great, talking, ideological Trojan horse of culture that these things don't matter?

As we waded deeper and deeper into the politics of perception, "the battle for hearts and minds," Jim Macdonald from the Canadian Labour Congress warmed up. Jim confessed that when he had received the invitation from the Arts Council to attend a cultural conference, he thought it was a conference about multiculturalism, and had prepared himself for such. In the mystical ways that consciousness blossoms, we knew Jim was right. We *were* talking about multiculturalism – but about a multiculturalism that included class identity as well as race and ethnicity. The issue of identity politics and its relationship to socialism became engaged at that time, to enter what would become a stormy marriage. Under the umbrella of the CLC, with the enthusiastic backing of Ontario Regional Director Doug Tobin and Wally Majesky and Mike Lyons of the Labour Council of Metropolitan Toronto, we set up a committee and called it the Labour, Arts and Media Working Group (LAMWG). I volunteered to help organize a conference on these topics, and D'Arcy Martin, who was education director for the United Steelworkers, offered to assist.

I knew D'Arcy because he and his wife Anita had two daughters, Danielle and Nyranne, who attended Friends Daycare Centre, which

Grayson had also attended before he graduated to grade one. During Grayson's last year at Friends, D'Arcy and I often met in the cloakroom a few minutes before the centre closed at five p.m. We exchanged only breathless pleasantries while squeezing the children into their snowsuits and searching for their boots and mittens. Since we were often the last parents to pick up our children, our clock-watching kids knew each other better than D'Arcy and I knew each other. I was familiar with D'Arcy's work, because I had heard him speak at a popular education conference years before and, at the time, been taken by his theories on adult education and class. He and I also had a number of acquaintances in common, like my Women's Press friends Rosemary Donegan and Dinah Forbes. Dinah and her husband Jonathan, with D'Arcy and Anita, were among the founding members of the Toronto-based Development Education Centre. D'Arcy and Rosemary, who had also worked at DEC for a time, had produced a series of beautiful posters for the CLC. Rosemary, an art historian, had combed through Canadian art and located several beautiful paintings depicting workers or their communities. Together they talked the CLC into publishing these works as a series of fine art posters called "Reflections of Our Labour." Copies of the posters are as common in union offices across the country today as were Group of Seven paintings in classrooms when I was in school. Like Bonnie, D'Arcy was another middle-class student who had rejected his parent's ambitions when he came face to face with student politics. He had all the enthusiasm, polish, and charm that comes with a boy's private school education. I began to realize I had a big crush on D'Arcy.

It is not just the rock 'n' roll world that has groupies and plaster casters, women who got their heroes to let them make plaster cast mouldings of their penises. What a trip that must have been for all concerned. During my short time in Vancouver I had been "in love" with the drummer from a band called Mother Tucker's Yellow Duck. I never made a plaster cast of his penis, but I did hang around the band's house and was quite satisfied to reflect in its glory. I had seen the same thing in Kincardine, when young women were always happy to follow my brother Robert's blues band around to wherever they played. Then there was the Lovin' Spoonful concert in Huntsville, Ontario, where I saw go-go girls dancing in the spotlight margins, high above the stage.

The corporate world, academic world, arts world, and religious world, wherever power politics play out, also have their plaster casters, and the left was not an exception. Italian sociologist Francesco Alberoni notes that it is not unusual in collectives to find groups of women who adore the same leader – that the "crowd" is a group of people who identify with each other and at the same time with the leader, usually a man. Having a crush on D'Arcy, of course, made me shy. It took some courage to ring his doorbell the evening I was invited to his house to work on plans for the Labour Council conference. In preparation I dressed carefully and arrived too early in his neighbourhood. I went to a nearby restaurant on Dupont Street and pulled out my journal. I became inhabited by the ghost of Mary Magdalen and wrote a short poem about the woman who washed Christ's feet, then dried them with her hair.

But although the thoroughly modern man who answered the door with a bottle of Windex in one hand and a rag in the other was not Jesus Christ, he might have been to me. He asked me to wait in the living room while he finished his household chores and put his children to bed. This gave me time to observe his big and bright renovated Victorian home, directly across from the Huron Street Public School. I noticed the white upholstered furniture and thought about the plastic my mother used to protect her hard-earned and hard-to-see-the-dirt brown couch and chairs. A welcoming fireplace was flanked by bookcases, crammed to the ceiling with dozens and dozens of hardcover books. It was nothing like my own place, with its haphazard collection of used furniture, makeshift bookcases, and paperbacks. D'Arcy summoned me upstairs to say good night to Danielle and Nyranne, who were as gracious as their father. Once his fatherhood responsibilities were fulfilled for the night, we went to work and began our arts and labour work, a job that would take us through the next six years.

The conference, "Arts and Labour: Working Partners," was held at the Steelworkers Hall on Cecil Street in Toronto in 1983. It attracted artists from a number of disciplines who already had informal connections with the labour movement, people like cartoonist and puppeteer Mike Constable, musician Arlene Mantle, playwright Steven Bush, filmmaker Laura Sky, and the activist writer Susan Meurer. We explored ways and means of integrating the arts more fully into labour's other struggles for better wages, working conditions, progressive legislation, and human rights.

Part of the job, as had been the case in the women's and human rights movements, would mean retrieving and highlighting working-class history and culture. We also committed ourselves to finding ways of encouraging workers to view the arts as a means of expressing their own ideas. An important piece of that lost working-class history, it turned out, was that cultural activities and the arts had already long been a part of the life of the labour movement. Music, theatre, and the visual arts had played important roles in building the confidence of working people and their unions until after the Second World War, when in the throes of the Cold War these activities were purged from mainstream union life. Only communists in the labour movement, the propaganda went, were interested in the arts; only communists were interested in expressing the ideas and concerns of workers. So it was a sign of better things to come when shortly after the conference the CLC presented a pilot, week-long arts-labour course for union activists and staff, which was soon adapted into a weekend course for labour councils across Ontario.

Susan Meurer first introduced me to the work and ideas of William Morris, the romantic poet, artist, and designer who was a leading socialist thinker and activist during Britain's industrial revolution. I found out that the wallpaper – with its flowers, fruits, and trellises – that had covered up the walls and brightened the small dark rooms in the Glasgow tenements I knew as a child had been the idea of this first poet of socialist thought. Morris applied the technology of the new printing press, until then the most powerful vehicle of industrial capitalist propaganda, to the task of bringing art and beauty to the homes of ordinary folk. He presented his vision of "the earthly paradise," the socialist dream, to people dislocated from the land and nature, people who had come to live in damp crowded slums and work for a pittance under dreadful conditions in the factories and mills of Britain. With a passion I dove into a huge paperback edition of E.P. Thompson's thundering biography of Morris.

Although Marx had articulated, in economic terms, the alienation created by the industrial revolution, and Freud had identified and charted the resulting neurosis in psychoanalytic terms, it seemed to me that Morris, both socialist and artist, understood images and symbols as more than clues to improving individual consciousness. Morris saw arts and crafts as vehicles into the sacred mine shafts of the collective soul. With his commitment to necessity *and* morality as engines of social change, Morris saw the potential of socialism as the highest expression of human life, lived with dignity and purpose. Morris thus joined Marx and Freud in my by then delightfully crowded men's room of consciousness.

In these years of new exploration into the mix of politics, art, and working-class culture, I grew immensely fond of Karl and Carole. We had regular evenings together, sitting around the big table in their home and studio on Bathurst Street, right near Toronto's Factory Theatre Lab. We gathered inside amidst their collections of union memorabilia, books, posters, hand-woven rugs, vintage cameras, and radios, as well as outdoors in the magnificent garden that Carole tends while Karl cooks. Whether inside or outside, their table was never quiet. It was a magnet for activists and artists from Australia, Britain, and across Canada. It was at Karl and Carole's table that I met video artists Kim Tomczak and Lisa Steele, culture critic and artist Clive Robertson, and filmmaker John Greyson. They debated socialism and life, art and organizing, and were intent on forming an artists' union in Canada.

We all used our own lives and backgrounds to explore ideas about our class and gender identities. We could agree that these identities were based on our common experience of relationships to power. I still have a line drawing I made of a woman's head exploding like a popcorn machine. The kernels of experience and learning I had been collecting were popping into a sense that I actually knew what I was talking about. Finally, and I think I was like the others in this respect, I was no longer memorizing Christian or Marxist or Freudian catechisms. I had tapped into my own experience-base, and it gave me a new and potent feeling, taking me way beyond my earlier assumption that I needed to change class allegiance in order to grow. We were entering the realm of identity and representational politics, rooted in the economic and class analysis we all brought with us into the discussions. As well, by fusing these ideas with feminism, another possibility opened to me – the potential and the freedom for a political analysis that I could finally call my own. If culture is an expression of our beliefs, hopes, and desires, and if I could learn to be proud of my working-class culture (not aspiring to middle-class measures of success), if I was learning to be proud about being a woman (not aspiring to be a man with tits), perhaps I could also find ways to stop being ashamed of my Catholic heritage as well.

Soul was a word I hadn't used much after leaving the church – except maybe when I had a yearning for the songs of Aretha Franklin or Otis Redding. I had been taught that we were all born with souls marked by original sin. The sacrament of baptism, which made us Catholics, erased that handicap. When we were kids the church used an illustration of milk bottles in the catechism to illustrate the soul. The milk bottle that could be said to be in a state of grace was pure white. Little, or venial, sins made black blotches in the milk. A damned soul was represented by a black milk bottle. Since there was no use crying over spilt milk, and since in the eyes of the church I had lost mine, the concept of soul had slipped right out of my mind.

In 1983, as I read Bruno Bettelheim's essay, "Freud and Man's Soul," I realized it had become more acceptable (fashionable, actually) in certain circles to admit you were seeing a psychiatrist than a priest or other spiritual director. Virginia Wolfe, Sylvia Plath, and Anne Sexton, as famous for their suicides as for their extraordinary insights and glorious works, were women's literary role models; the message was that a conscious woman was a mad woman. You could get sympathy and comfort if you said you were losing your mind, but you could clear a room if you said you were losing your soul. Bettelheim argues that although Freud was an atheist, he had a deep concern for the spiritual and that Freud's English translators corrupted his intent. By sticking to the early stages of his theories, with their inclination to science and medicine, and by disregarding his later holistic work, which was more concerned with broader cultural and human issues, including matters of the soul, Freud's interpreters promoted the medical model. A whole new profession was built and prospered on the misrepresentation that the human mind, like the body, was something that could be examined, measured, and cured, for a price. "When Freud talked about an urge to return to the womb, he had a lot more in mind than a biological journey," Bettelheim argued. "Who," he asked, "would want to return to a uterus?"

Bettelheim's list of errors in translation from the original German was fascinating and informative, especially his argument about the resulting elimination of Freud's references to the soul. In *The Interpretation of Dreams*, for example, Freud had said that the "dream is the result of the activity of our own soul." The word "soul" was translated as "mind." Bettelheim maintained, long before the introduction of Prozac, that a fundamental dishonesty, which served only too well the purposes of the aggressive U.S. medical establishment, was at play. The world of psychoanalysis that Freud had opened up was too lucrative to leave in the hands of the non-medically trained. The new breed of mind-doctors and pharmaceutical companies was happier with mysterious, difficult language than with the more poetic and spiritual language of the author whose ideas they plundered. The word "I" became "ego." The word "it," meaning everything external to the individual became "id." Although now part of the common language, the word "superego" was also a cooked-up term.

I suppose I have Bruno Bettelheim and D'Arcy Martin to thank for giving me the impetus to take my first run at the "Catholic Question" and seek spiritual direction. After D'Arcy and his wife Anita had separated, D'Arcy suggested that we might develop our work relationship into something more intimate. I was tempted. I didn't especially like being a single mother, and I longed to settle down. I saw in D'Arcy a man who liked children, who seemed to know what he was doing with his life, and who appreciated Grayson. But I had serious doubts.

I called the Newman Centre, a Roman Catholic Resource Centre on the University of Toronto campus, and made an appointment to talk my situation over with a young priest, a friend of Steven Bush. Over the next few weeks the priest and I spent many hours talking about our lives and sharing attitudes about the Catholic faith. I dragged up every anti-Catholic cliché I knew and listed all my grievances, from the authoritarian education I had received as a child to what I regarded as the horrors of the anti-woman hierarchy. I put as heroic and rational a spin on all of this as possible – on the "sins" I had committed since I left the church. In so doing, I made a half-hearted kind of reconciliation. It used to be called confession.

The Catholic Church has a beautiful concept called "The Seven Gifts of the Spirit" – the gifts a person can receive from God, as he or she moves through life. The priest, a Vietnam veteran, inspired me to use the seven gifts of the spirit as a means of doing a personal inventory. In support of this decision of mine, my friend Jennifer Palen gave me a number of articles she had clipped. One was by Andrew M. Greeley on the spirituality and sacramentality of Bruce Springsteen's lyrics; another was by the radical Catholic theologian Matthew Fox rejecting the concept of original sin in favour of original blessing. Given my soul-sickness, and the great temptation D'Arcy represented, I needed to get some sense of my spiritual readiness for a new relationship. Although I had never acknowledged it or given her any thanks, throughout most of our sporadic relationship Jennifer had always played the role of spiritual director. She did it with such a light and generous hand that I barely noticed it.

Sitting alone in my kitchen one evening, I read the articles and began to make notes on a foolscap pad, dividing the page into two columns marked "assets" and "liabilities." In the asset column, I wrote the word "piety," the first gift of the spirit. At first, because I had rejected the church, I didn't feel that I could count that as one of my gifts, but when I really thought about it, I had to admit that I did believe in some kind of higher power. Much to my surprise, I did have a certain amount of piety. At the beginning of this spiritual journey, I tried to justify that penchant to my friend Shelley Acheson by pointing to my forearm. "I know there is more to all this than this heavy bone and flesh," I said. The second gift of the spirit is knowledge. I put that down in the asset column. But the third gift, "understanding," is not the same as knowledge. Since I was just beginning to process the knowledge I had been acquiring, I put knowledge in the liability column. That was the gift I had desperately sought all my life, and it still seemed to allude me.

The other three gifts of the spirit were problematic too. Fortitude is the courage to face pain or trouble. I was someone in the habit of running from pain, although I was not afraid to make trouble. I listed that one in both columns. As for the sixth gift, wisdom – the good judgement we gain from experience – I was full of bravado, but I didn't think I was particularly wise. Nor did I feel justified in claiming the seventh gift – reverence. I was still too suspicious, too angry, and too fearful to experience reverence and the awe and love that flow from it. I had glimpses of what I thought to be authentic reverence, like when I had touched my pregnant belly and later when I had held Grayson when he was born. And I had lots of experience with groupie-style or unauthentic reverence, especially for men. But a generalized experience of reverence was not something I had much claim to.

At the end of this simple spiritual exercise I decided I was not ready to enter another relationship. The priest agreed. I still had a lot of spiritual work to do before I made any more big life decisions. I turned my attention back to Grayson and my work, with a resulting satisfaction and peace of mind. My priorities would be being a mother, the work that I did, and political organizing. I now had a spiritual agenda of my own, as well as a political one. I would work on the gaining of understanding, fortitude, wisdom, and reverence, and I would continue to work in the arts and labour movement.

In a 1984 *Our Times* article, Karl Beveridge wrote a summary of his theories about the working class and its connections to the arts. The mass media pay people decent wages, he said, but give them little or no say in what they produce. In the fine arts people have some control over what they make, but get paid little for it. For this reason, professional artists get to do what they want, but their work is generally small-scale, and rarely seen. In either case the audience for the arts counts for "absolutely nothing. Zero."

We had the opportunity to do something about this – put some of this theory into practice that same year, during a bitter unionizing drive at the Eaton's department store chain. The Retail, Wholesale and Department Store Union and a group of artists staged a gala support performance at Massey Hall in Toronto in May. The event, called "We Don't Shop at Eaton's," featured music, readings, and performances by writers and artists, including Rick Salutin and R.H. Thompson. We proved that the labour movement and its friends could fill a house as big as Massey Hall, if the artists cared about a working-class audience. That same year I was invited to attend Mayfest in Scotland, where I saw that what had happened in just one night at Massey Hall took place for three weeks every year in my hometown during Glasgow's festival of the arts. Mayfest, the brain-child of the Scottish Arts Council and the Scottish Trade Union Congress, was a financial boon for the economically depressed city as well as a successful cultural reclamation. It had, for instance, the Scottish Symphony performing work composed to honour working people. Every main-stage theatre in the city was politically alert – recognizing not just the proud working-class traditions of the townsfolk but also the struggles of peoples in El Salvador and Nicaragua. Scottish writers were reverting to their own dialects. In community centres across the city, professional artists were working with local people to produce new and exciting works.

Like the revival of working-class culture in Liverpool in the 1960s and 1970s, the popular culture generated by the success of the Beatles, the more literary contributions of the Liverpool poets, and the growing international acclaim for the works of novelist Catherine Cookson, in Scotland sales soared as a new and broader arts market cast its vote for popular culture. As Alex Clarke, the arts officer of the Scottish Trade Union Congress, walked me through the festival that he had helped found, I saw a new opening for my work, and life. Perhaps something that I had thought had been lost or broken long ago could indeed be mended: the soul of the postwar working-class.

11

Death

When Marx was thinking about history, he is thinking in Hegelian terms. History is the sphere in which spirit is realizing itself in the world. It is realizing itself always in relation to nature. Here appears the distinction between spirit and nature. Nature is what it is and is not what it is not. A stone is a stone and not something else. But man is self-conscious, and self-consciousness is divided against itself. Man can always stand above himself and make himself what he is not. Every action is a project to the future, in which we negate what we are now. Therefore, man both is and is not what he is. Spirit, then, has a different logic from the logic of identity proper to nature. History is the coming to be of spirit in the world.

George Grant, *Philosophy in the Mass Age* (1959)

WHILE ALCOHOL HUMOURS the spirit, death challenges it. Shortly after my return from Mayfest in Scotland, Pat Schulz lost her fight with bone cancer. As I kept watch in Pat's Garden of Gethsemane, I found myself praying. In the world before the pain, had Pat known I was praying she would have given me a lecture about rationality. She was as rational as I was romantic. In the world before the pain she would have argued with me or laughed and sang the protest song about getting "pie in the sky when you die."

I could have argued back, what's the difference between the work we do as socialists and prayer? Aren't our fights for justice over greed, for the well-being of children, for the honour of women's forms of prayer? Chants for socialists? My Catholic teachers would have called these battles struggles of faith, hope, and love, the greatest of these, of course, being love. But I would more likely have avoided this discussion. I knew that religion had been used and abused as "the opium of the masses," but I had nothing against the idea of God herself. People either believe in a God or they don't. In those days I still kept my ideas about spirituality in the closet and hadn't yet "come out." Pat and I could agree, however, that our kind of activism was more than a fight for material gain, much more than a fight for the redistribution of wealth. Romantic or rational, there was a new world for men, women, and children to be created, and the redistribution of wealth was one of the ways to achieve it. But much could also be done along the way. We were moving from consciousness-raising to politics, with the idea of going on from politics to something better – be it democracy, William Morris's earthly paradise, or Tommy Douglas's New Jerusalem.

The phrase "the dictatorship of the proletariat," however, had a bad ring to it by then for me, and I had stopped using it. Some of us differentiated ourselves from men we knew in the left who needed to view class struggle as an end in itself, and in so doing turned their political practice into progressive-sounding totalitarianisms. We were not happy with dictatorships of any ideological stripe. In conversations and musings that had taken place over coffee around Pat's lively round table, in the tiny sunroom of her Bain Avenue apartment, we talked about how feminism had to be the empathetic identification with the suffering of all women.

By that time we had the advantage of a flourishing of new women's writing and production that was bringing forth all kinds of wit and wisdom, blind rage, and analysis. Strong feminist voices, like that of the

Toronto-based performance artists The Clichettes and journalist and activist Michele Landsberg, were being heard, produced, and published by mainstream publishing houses. In *Women and Children First*, which appeared around this time, Michele Landsberg reflected on how good ideas can be turned into iron laws that "shape us instead of our shaping them." Michele tried to imagine a matriarchal society in which housewives and mothers were amply rewarded with fat salaries, pensions, bonuses, and tax credits, and doctors would be expected to work all their lives out of sheer love and Hippocratic duty. Any suggestion of pay for doctors would spark righteous indignation: "I'm insulted at the idea of being paid! I care for my patients out of love, and consider myself fortunate to be loved in return. That's all the pay I need."

In 1983 during the International Women's Day celebrations in Toronto, an ugly incident arose when a Jewish woman tried to infuse a discussion about Palestine liberation with feminism. The woman was silenced. With Laura Weintraub, Pat and I wrote public letters condemning the silencing and calling for support of all women who struggled for peace. We pleaded with our sisters to transcend inherited ideologies – especially those that wore religious disguises. We insisted that socialist feminists climb the patriarchal barricades and forge our own values, make our own linkages. In our "prayer" for the Palestinian and Israeli people, we also prayed for ourselves. But in 1984, in Pat's room in the Grace Hospital on Church Street, in Toronto, we were no longer safe at the musing table. We were in the world of suffering. The time for all serious and even whimsical talk about philosophy and politics was over, reduced to water and morphine. Conversations with my "wise woman" Pat were over. She was too ill to engage.

I had never witnessed death before. I had seen my maternal grandfather in his coffin, which took up most of the space in the living room of my grandmother's small house in Penilee, Glasgow. The heavy curtains were drawn, the room damp with flowers and sobbing. It was a fleeting glimpse of death, for I was hurried away. But I had not seen him die. By the time my grandmothers died, they did so quietly and invisibly on the other side of the Atlantic Ocean. Although their deaths saddened me, because I never saw them in their coffins, I have only living images of them.

I had seen emotional suffering, and I had seen physical suffering. But I had no experience with the degree of suffering that cancer brings, and the finality of morphine. My decision to pray, I want to say, was not conscious; it just happened as I reconciled myself with the ultimate fragility of the human body and the limits of my ability to negotiate with death. The Ash Wednesdays of my childhood, of dust and mortality, drifted back. Singing the requiem mass in the choir at our Lady of Sorrows in Petawawa came back to me.

Standing beside Pat's bed, there was no argument I could make. No medicine to take. No appeal process. No legislation that could be changed. No revolution to be called for. It wasn't like the other times when Pat and Laura and I had fought off death and won; when we had the luxury of an enemy we could identify and a wrong we could try to right. So, privately and uninterrupted, I took refuge and comfort in my long submerged and secret language. We had done all we could. There was nothing left but to pray.

Several months before Pat was finally admitted to the Grace Hospital, when the chemotherapy had stopped working, her doctors shifted her onto an oral treatment. She was told the side effects were minimal, although she might experience some weakness due to changes in the calcium level of her blood. Her Princess Margaret Hospital doctor said that if she ran into trouble she should call immediately for admission to the hospital. When Pat went to pick up the drug and another one that was supposed to minimize the chances of pain, she found out that the aspirin-based pain killers she was using couldn't be used with the second drug. She was prescribed an alternative.

By midnight the pain started in her lower back. She took the new pain killer and a muscle relaxant and tried to sleep but she couldn't. She took more and still couldn't sleep. By 3 a.m. she was taking three Tylenol No. 3 every four hours and two Robaxin. They made her dizzy and numbed her face. By 7:30 Saturday morning she called the Princess Margaret Hospital and asked to be admitted for a needle. She was told that the Princess Margaret Hospital had no emergency department. There was no way she could be admitted. Since it was the weekend, she couldn't reach her doctor at the clinic. All she was offered was a call to her pharmacist for stronger pain pills. When I went to the pharmacy to pick up the prescription, I was told the doctor had prescribed an aspirin-based drug she couldn't take. After a few more calls, I returned to Pat's bedside with a narcotic and an anti-nausea pill to keep it down. But that didn't work either.

After a couple of hours of more agony Laura called one of our neighbours, a doctor who lived in the Bain Co-op. He said he couldn't give Pat anything else until four hours after the previous drug, but he did manage to get the phone number for Pat's GP, who confirmed what we had already been told. When, four hours later, the second dose failed to make any difference, we realized that here we were: three lay people trying to deal with six different chemicals we knew nothing about. We called an ambulance and headed unannounced to Mount Sinai Hospital. The emergency department was packed. Patients lay on stretchers, separated only by curtains. There were no pillows in the whole emergency section. We looked through cupboards ourselves until we found two old ones, which we used to prop up Pat's head and try to comfort her while she waited. At 11 p.m. Pat received relief. She had been in agony for twenty-three hours.

One sunny morning near the end of her life I found Pat sitting in a wheel chair at the end of a corridor, parked at a window facing south down Church Street. There was a little bird singing in a cage beside her. When I spoke Pat's name, she turned and looked at me, but right through me. The warmth that had always welcomed my visits was gone. I was a stranger. I knew then that she had already left and would never be back.

But her body kept fighting. On the evening her body died she was taking a few breaths in a stop-and-go fashion. Just when I thought she wouldn't breath again, she would surprise me by inhaling and exhaling again. She struggled like this for what seemed like hours. Each time she stopped I would whisper to her: "Let go, Pat, just let go." I prayed for the courage to stay with her. I also made a prayer for intersession – to put in a good word for the woman who had taught me so much and had loved me much more than I was capable of loving myself. Pat's body slipped away from the pain late in the evening. I left the hospital with her daughter Katheryne, only sixteen years old. Katheryne's father had died when she was only two, and now she had lost her mother.

Most mother's lives – including that of my own mother, who worked outside the home all her life – are shaped by the moral and emotional choices they make and have made for them about sex, children, and family. My mother's choices were limited by the times she lived in, as were mine, although I benefited from the cultural, economic, and reproductive-technological freedoms of my times. One of the tragedies, of course, was the separation that these times created between my mother and me. My mother experienced all my new ideas as personal rejections. After sacrificing my relationship with my mother to go in what I considered to be new directions, I spent a lot of time seeking her blessing, which she, in turn, withheld. Eventually we reached a truce, but it was not until I had become a mother myself.

As one way of making amends for my part in that nasty little mother/daughter war I started to write again, this time turning my mind to theatre. I had moved away from my purely romantic ideas about art and realized that writing could be both personally *and* politically useful. I began work on *Glow Boys*, a performance piece, loosely based on my family's experience as workers at the Douglas Point nuclear reactor.

Glow Boys, it seemed, was a perfect model for a community arts project. I would work with a group of professional visual artists and actors.

Karl Beveridge and Carole Condé were interested, as were actor Maja Ardal and producer and director Don Bouzak. It would be a collective creation. We would live in the town of Kincardine during the summer of 1985 and invite musicians and other local artists to join us. In the process, we would learn from each other. The research for the play was done with the support of a number of the Douglas Point workers, who generously provided us with stories and photographs that we integrated into the multimedia script.

But, as often happens, people on the team had varied agendas – different ideas of what the play was about and how we should work. Some of the contributors were environmentalists and anti-nuclear activists, and brought that emphasis to the content. Others were interested in working-class culture and the power of the union to influence the direction of public energy policy. The feminists among us were concerned about the lives of working-class women in the family and in single-industry towns. Conflicts arose over money and vision for the project – about whether the "professionals" amongst us should be paid union scale, in keeping with union principles, for instance. If Pat had been alive, I would have called her and she would have given me good advice on how to balance these forces in the script I was to write. As an alternative, I turned frequently to a nice bottle of Ballantine's to help me cope. Tensions mounted and unpleasantly culminated one evening during rehearsals when one of the actors threw a chair at the director. Still, we managed to pull together and in the end I had the sense that we were all trying to do our best. The play was performed first in August during the Canadian Labour Congress family week in Port Elgin, then for two nights at the Kincardine Pavilion in September.

The play looked at the nuclear history of the area from the perspectives of three generations of the same family. The elders, Duncan and Pandora, represented my parents and spoke from the age of optimism, embodying the almost neomystical postwar dreams hung on the potential of nuclear power. I was interested in the morality of the nuclear industry and the limits of purely scientific thought. The mystical aspect of nuclear power, because it was false to begin with, was lost on the next generation, whose dreams were replaced by the more material fruits of the industry, represented by the gleaming Harley Davidson motorcycle, belonging to my brother Robert, that dominated the set. The future was imagined in the character of the grandchild of the pioneers, speaking to the audience from the year 2000. The grandchild is a tour guide at what is, by then, called the Bruce Nuclear Power Development Museum and Adventure Park. The play anticipated the decline of the nuclear industry.

The Kincardine audiences liked the play – the local weekly newspaper gave it a positive review, and a CUPE union steward, Brad Kirkconnell, handwrote a review, copied it, and posted it throughout the plant. But by far the best review was my mother's: she liked it.

Back in Toronto, even though I was exhausted from the emotional and financial pressures of the *Glow Boys* production, I joined up with many of the same people and began organizing the first Mayworks Festival of Working People and the Arts. As well, somehow in the aftermath of Pat's death I had forgotten all my good intentions about not embarking on a new relationship with a man and got closely involved with D'Arcy. As I was becoming more and more accepting and proud of my working-class roots, and more comfortable with my cultural Catholicism – that part of me that thought and acted like a Catholic, even though I was not formally connected to the church – I had fallen in love (or hero worship) again. But I couldn't just fall in love like other people, I had to justify it in political terms. I read *Falling in Love*, by Francesco Alberoni, a book heralded as presenting "a revolutionary new way of thinking about a universal experience." Alberoni called falling in love "the nascent state of a collective movement involving two individuals."

A certain unreality on my part, as well as our approaches to childrearing and my emerging sense of identity, would eventually put D'Arcy and me on a collision course. In the bleak moments, which were few and far between, we waged open class and philosophical warfare in our kitchen.

At first he was patient and understanding, but no amount of understanding could mask the basic differences between us.

Take childrearing. His model was rooted in 1950s middle-class America, the decade that has been so mythologized as the time of normalcy. Even though he had lived an alternative lifestyle, his approach to childrearing was decidedly different from mine – though to say that I had an approach to childrearing would be an exaggeration. I played it by ear. D'Arcy spent hours ferrying Danielle and Nyranne around to special lessons and events, as if "perfection" was attainable in parenting. But this particular kind of parental guidance, it seemed to me, came with a huge price tag, one that I had never been able to afford. I was more informal when I had the time after work and all the housework was done. Putting a record on the turntable – maybe something like Bob Seeger's "Like a Rock" – and encouraging Danielle's bent for dancing was my idea of leading them along.

The other difference between D'Arcy and me, and on this we agreed, was his confidence, one of the intangible gifts of "class privilege." My fears, and there were many, were based in my lack of class privilege. As always seems the case, this pat analysis was too simplistic. We were equally vulnerable to each other's powers in our own ways. D'Arcy had an intellectual energy and discipline, for example, that amazed me. When I think of our early times together, I picture him as the driver in a speedboat. I am the white-knuckled novice on water skis behind him, teeth clenched in smile, expecting to wipe out at any second. As it turned out, he felt much the same way – except that he thought I was in the driver's seat and he was the accident waiting to happen.

My barely articulated spirituality and my better understood class rage would sometimes surface like the lumbering Loch Ness monster, at the most surprising and inappropriate times. While D'Arcy could bless the working-class in me, he couldn't relate to the anger that came with it or to my more spooky cultural Catholic parts. But in between our battles – which erupted every six months or so, usually when I had had too much to drink — we had a lot of fun. I had so much fun, in fact, that I forgot I still had a drinking problem and that Grayson wasn't interested in playing family with us.

Like the little old lady who lived in a shoe, I was trying to smooth affairs over in a home that now had a cast of challenging young people rotating through it regularly. Like me, D'Arcy shared custody. Every two weeks Nyranne and Danielle lived with us. There were piano lessons and practices, jazz and tap dancing lessons and rehearsals, public-speaking competitions, figure-skating classes, and school projects. Every three weeks Grayson lived with us, and over the course of one year Grayson's best friend Ramel also lived with us on the same rotating basis, after his parents separated and his mother moved home to Jackson, Mississippi, to find her feet. Katheryne Schulz, although she had her own apartment, was a regular visitor.

Sometimes the children's stays overlapped. When Ramel was reunited with his mother and left Toronto, Grayson missed his "brother," his breakdancing partner, terribly. So did I, because I liked Ramel and he was head and shoulders above the new friends Grayson soon had marching home with him — big, surly fellows with shaved heads wearing eighteen-hole Doc Marten boots. Soon I was getting regular calls from Grayson's school telling me he had skipped classes. I was so preoccupied with my work and all this family life that I didn't heed the early warning signs of those calls or of the Doc Marten boots.

My daily preoccupations also meant that when my mother became ill, the seriousness of her condition didn't sink in. My mother wasn't a complainer. She called one day to let me know that she would be in Toronto to see the Pope, who was saying mass at St. Michael's Cathedral. I agreed to meet my parents in the coffee shop at the Bond Place Hotel, where they would be staying. She was so excited the day I saw her that her hands were trembling. When she tried to take her medication she dropped the pills on the floor. I got on my hands and knees and crawled under the table to collect them for her. My mother had seen the Pope and his entourage from her hotel window overlooking the cathedral. The next time I saw her was just before Christmas, when I visited her in the Kincardine Hospital. The last time was three months later in the Owen Sound Hospital's intensive care unit. My mother was plugged into life-support machines and never regained consciousness after suffering an aneurysm. She died at 3 p.m. on Good Friday, 1986.

Uncle Ronnie and Aunt Bea came from Toronto for the funeral. My mother's sister Aunt Mary came from Scotland. Another sister, Aunt Margaret, came from Brooklyn. We placed a Macleod hunting tartan scarf that my brother had given to her around the neck of her white blouse. My mother, the young girl who had become a woman on the streets of old Govan, looked like a clan chief. We made a tape of her favourite music, which played during the visiting hours. Over and over I heard Paul McCartney's "Mull of Kintyre." Visitors came and went. My father wore sunglasses. A funeral Mass was held at St. Anthony's, and the priest called death "a sting."

We couldn't immediately bury my mother, because the ground was frozen. While her body waited for the coming of spring thaw, I switched to automatic pilot and returned to work on the Mayworks Festival. Mayworks, a group of us had decided, would take the artistic expression of working-class people seriously. I argued that we could look at the very act of participating in a union as a magnificent form of abstract art practised by working people. In taking unionism seriously, workers constantly helicopter up from the anti-union cultures in which they live and away from the back-breaking or soul-destroying landscape of their workplaces. They make a leap of spirit in even imagining a workplace in which social responsibility, gender and racial equality, personal dignity, and cultural democracy are as important as production and profit.

Mayworks would recognize the art of living and working and learning. We would promote the poetry of workers like the CAW's Ron Dickson and exhibit the photographs and paintings and drawings of people like CUPE's Vincenzo Pietropaolo and activist Mike Constable. We would listen to the music of singer/songwriter Arlene Mantle. Mayworks would be a crossroads at which work and creativity could meet.

The psychotherapist and writer Thomas Moore calls this idea "the sacred arts of life." Broadly, Moore defines the arts as that which invites us to contemplate:

> In that moment of contemplation, art intensifies the presence of the world. We see it more vividly and more deeply. The emptiness that many people complain dominates their lives comes in part from the failure to let the world in, to perceive it and to engage it fully. Naturally, we'll feel empty if everything we do slides past without sticking. As we have seen, art arrests attention, an important service to the soul. . . . Living artfully, therefore, might require something as simple as pausing.

But paycheques aren't issued for pausing. Workers sell their time to their employers and are discouraged from pausing, never mind thinking about anything other than the work they have been hired to perform. Unions, however, could create time for thinking, for the imagination, and Mayworks and other cultural activities could help to create that political space for working-class people.

At the beginning, though, the Mayworks Festival was just an idea some of us had about taking art and cultural activity from its low position on labour's agenda and raising it up to a place where it could be recognized for its political and social importance. To take that idea and make it into reality took the work of an extraordinarily creative organizer and administrator, Su Ditta. In the time after my mother's death I simply couldn't cope with helping to pull it all together. Su came in to work on the festival as its first co-ordinator; and she really made it work, kept it from fading away on the drawing boards.

My mother's burial didn't take place until the end of April, when the Mayworks Festival was in full swing, and all the tulip bulbs she had planted in the beds in front of the house on Mechanics Avenue in Kincardine were a fury of red blooms.

When my mother died, my family asked me to write her epitaph but I could think of nothing to say. I stared at a blank piece of paper for two days in a room at the Broadway Motel in Kincardine that D'Arcy and I had moved into while we made "the arrangements." When I finally managed to put my pen to paper the only words that came out were "nobody left to blame." Then I realized that I had already written my mother's epitaph. An excerpt from *Glow Boys*, my real tribute to my mother, was performed at the CLC Convention during the first Mayworks Festival, the same week of the Chernobyl disaster.

While writing *Glow Boys*, I had never heard of Chernobyl in the Northern Ukraine, on the Pripyat River. But by the time my father sat with Alex Clark, visiting from Glasgow's Mayfest to watch that performance, we all knew that on April 26, ten miles to the north of that city, at the Chernobyl nuclear power plant, engineers had initiated an uncontrolled chain reaction in the core of the reactor. Thirty-one people, all firefighters or workers at the plant, died immediately, and hundreds of others suffered from severe radiation sickness. The disaster devastated farming economies in eastern and northern Europe and contaminated the lives of the people who lived near the plant. Scientists estimated that there would be 20,000 to 40,000 related deaths from cancer over the following sixty years.

Since I had written the script for *Glow Boys*, and since my mother had approved of it, I think I can say that both of us – she who was born in 1917 and I in 1948 and named after her – finally had the chance to speak our minds in 1986. It may have been too late to make any difference to my mother, but it was not too late for the daughter she had given life to.

Last night the sun dropped out of the clouds like a fresh egg
yolk. It hovered like it didn't weigh more than a feather, then it
sank. The way old people get when they're dying. The way
anything gets when it's dying. The second the sun disappears
– if you turn your head to the right – you see the first cool
twinkles of the nuclear plant. I swear there's someone in there
who pushes a button that says – "Beat the sun at its own
game." But it can't be done, as far as I'm concerned. The plant
is garish. It reminds me of the Titanic on its maiden voyage.
Cheap. Too easy. It can't hold a candle to the real thing. It's
too cold . . . but there's no denying its attraction. Sometimes
the plant really is spectacular. Sometimes I want to reach out
and touch it. I feel it buzzing in my veins. Sometimes I dream
about it glowing cold and bright. My husband has a framed
photograph of it in our bedroom. Where we should have my
crucifix.

One night I dreamt I was standing at the foot of the cross
on Calvary. I was holding a jar of atomic fireflies in my hand.
I couldn't see what was going on but I knew something was
dying. It was dark. In the dark I could hear someone sobbing.
I could hear the comforting sounds a mother is supposed to
make.

My husband used to give me books to read. I think he
wanted to convert me. I think he wanted me to become a true-
believer like him. But I never wanted to know nuclear. I told
my husband I wanted to stick to my own God . . . I'm not a
heretic, I told him. I'd rather spend my time taking care of my
garden or making things, like curtains.

12

Hitching a Ride with the Auto Workers

BETWEEN MY MOTHER'S DEATH and a job working with the Canadian Auto Workers' union in 1987, I stayed close to my kitchen and small garden on Garnock Avenue. Basically, I was in mourning. I put down the books I had been reading – political theory, history, women's literature – and turned to the lives of saints – St. Catherine of Sienna, St. Augustine, St. Ignatius Loyola. I studied the mysteries of the rosary – the joyful, the sorrowful, and the glorious – and the Stations of the Cross. I was searching for clues about the faith that had given my mother her strength. I found images that resonated and echoed, concepts long ago buried but, when unearthed, were as alive as the roses of St. Teresa, known as the little flower. I found myself writing poetry as if my life depended on it, and from time to time had acute panic attacks.

I had bought a used Nikkormat camera and switched from Polaroid to 35-millimetre film. Since I had a disorganized collection of slides, prints, and contact sheets – shots of friends and family, the work I had done, and the people I met along the way – I decided to sort through those files. I knew a woman who ran a small gallery in the Yorkville area and asked her to look at my work. Ruth Weller liked my shots of women best. I matched a dozen or so of these images with some of the poetry I had been writing and had my first solo exhibition at the Weller Potowsky Gallery on Scollard Street during the 1987 Mayworks Festival. The exhibition, "Natural Woman," included portraits of the women in my family, my sister Janis Shewfelt, my sister-in-law Susan Macleod with her second son, Joel, in her arms, Laura Weintraub, and Grayson's step-mother Hilary Salter.

Buoyed by the work of pulling the exhibition together, by summer I felt confident enough to apply for a temporary position in the communications department of the Ontario Public Service Employees Union, supporting the union's public campaigns on issues from the human rights of welfare recipients and mental health patients to the preservation of the provincial park system. At OPSEU I met Mary Rowles, a feminist who, at the time, headed the women's program. Mary pulled the first OPSEU all-women team together for "Making It Public," a campaign to fight the privatization of public services. Since public service workers could not publicly support candidates in elections, the campaign was a step towards challenging the law that denied political rights to public-sector workers by putting the question of privatization to all the candidates. That summer election eventually saw the defeat of the forty-year Conservative reign in Ontario. It was exhilarating to work with OPSEU members across the province, and with organizers like Jill Morgan and Kay McDonald.

At home Grayson was on a rampage. He shaved his head, punched holes in his bedroom wall, smashed the glass in his bedroom window, and left the shards on his floor. He branded his telephone with cigarette burns. He shattered his records, demolished his stereo. He pinned a picture of Adolf Hitler on his wall. Then he met a "Chelsea Girl," Samantha, three years older, who also shaved her head and wore Doc Martens. They talked white power. As he transformed himself into a hard-line fourteen-year-old skinhead, the two of us began a slow descent into a three-year ideological and emotional battle of wills.

I won't try to talk for Grayson, for his side of this story is his to tell, but for me it seemed there was nothing I could do to break his fall. D'Arcy, for good reason, was appalled and began to withdraw from me and to take steps to protect Danielle and Nyranne from the ugly crossfire. I don't think he was afraid of physical violence. I think he was afraid of the anti-Semitism and racism that was part and parcel of the skinhead subculture.

Switching to survival mode, I began to make preparations for single motherhood again, determined to hang onto my son.

Some mornings, waiting at Bloor and Yonge to catch the subway north
to Davisville and the OPSEU headquarters, I would lean my head against
the cool tiled wall of the platform to get my mind away from the idea of
jumping in front of the train, which some days seemed to be a deadly magnet. Through those days I managed to fight the increasingly intense panic
attacks by tapping – a trick I had learned in prenatal classes. During my
labour, before Grayson made his first appearance in the world, I had
tapped out, a hundred times, the tune to the nursery rhyme *"Bobby
Shafto's/gone to sea/silver buckles/on his knee/he'll be back/to marry me/
bonnie Bobby Shafto."*

During the OPSEU period I also put Charlie Chaplin's song *"Smile
though your heart is aching/smile even though it's breaking"* to full use. I pre-
tended that all was well, and I smiled. I also put out the word that I needed
a full-time job. In the past, time had been good to me, like when I stumbled
into the beginnings of the Women's Press, so again I placed my faith in
time. Within a few weeks I was asked to send a resumé and samples of my
work to the Canadian Auto Workers, to me the Camelot of the labour
movement. Peggy Nash, the communications director, needed an assistant. Bob White, the president, didn't interview me, but he did phone to
tell me I had the job. "I'm a bastard to work for," he warned. "You don't
frighten me," I lied.

Old ideas die hard. I was still in the habit of turning mortal men into
gods. The legendary Bob White was another idol of mine – the working-
class hero who, like King Arthur, had drawn the sword from the stone
when he led his union out of its international parent organization, the
UAW. With the members he had made history by founding an independent
Canadian union in the auto industry. I was not the only one who loved
him. Most of the members loved him, and the media did too.

What distinguished Bob from all the other labour leaders I had worked
with was that he loved the media too. He understood the media. Like the

auto companies, the media are owned by giant corporations, but operated on a day-to-day basis by workers. Bob respects workers. Although media corporations are in the business of selling ink and airtime, just as car companies are in the business of selling cars, workers are workers and they know a good job from a lousy one. Bob made their jobs easy. As CAW president he was not only an imaginative and tough negotiator, but he was also a snappy dresser, gifted with a great sense of humour, and fast with the language – a poet, in fact, of the thirty-second sound bite. On his way into one particularly difficult set of negotiations he quipped that he was "wading into an alligator swamp in bare feet." The more the public's affection for Bob grew, however, the more resentful his opponents in the labour movement became.

Bob White sold newspapers. Other labour leaders no doubt loved their members, but they distrusted media. And the Beatles are right: "the love you take is equal to the love you make." In his Willowdale court, and on the evening news, Bob was a noble leader and a mighty warrior. His brave knights included Bob Nickerson and Buzz Hargrove. The most unlikely knight of them all was the professorial Sam Gindin, the union's research director, the academic force in the Bob White administration. Another strength that distinguished Bob from other labour leaders of the day was that he respected intellectuals. He recognized the power of connecting his members with workers in the left-wing academic community. Sam was the link.

When I joined the CAW staff, the union was taking the labour lead in the charge against the free-trade agreement. Bob Nickerson, known as "Nick," was the CAW officer I came to know best. Nick, like Bob, was a tough negotiator with a memory like a steel trap and a remarkable skill with numbers. He didn't need to write things down. Fortunately for Nick, I never treated him like a God. He was a brother. This saved him from the big fall from grace that always happened when I stepped on the clay feet of the men I deified.

I had met Nick when he co-chaired the original Ontario Federation of Labour's Women's Committee. Only members of the OFL Executive

Board could chair standing committees, and because there were no women on the board at the time, Nick and Moe Keck from the Steelworkers got the job. Affirmative action – to get women into leadership roles in the labour movement – was at the top of the first Women's Committee agenda. Nick had taken great delight in showing women the ropes. He knew things were rocky at home for me, and sometimes though not often gave me a shoulder to cry on. He wanted me to toughen up, knowing, as I realized quickly enough myself, that the CAW's world was a hard place to live in. But Nick encouraged me to stay there long enough to accomplish a few things I had always wanted to do – like finding ways to integrate the arts and artists into the union's education and communication campaigns – as well as one thing I knew, by then, I had to do – quit drinking.

I flew to Newfoundland on the first day of the CAW job to begin work on the union's contentious campaign to organize the fishery workers. Under Richard Cashin, fishery workers had decided to leave the International United Food and Commercial Workers to form a new union under the roof of the CAW. The UFCW called it "raiding," a mortal sin in the house of labour. The final decision would be made by a vote of the members. I was to write a story for *Solidarity*, the union's magazine, and help design a media campaign to promote the CAW to fishery workers – plant, inshore, and deep sea. I know that the interunion battle that followed touched almost every community in the province of Newfoundland, for I visited a good number of them during the campaign. And it shook the house of labour, hauling the submerged issues of union democracy and Canadian autonomy right to the surface and hardening competitive resentments of the CAW into full-blown ideological and personal hatred.

In the three years I worked for that union the pace never slowed. The work would take me across Canada as well as to Africa and Nicaragua. I would play a part – providing media and communications backup – in negotiations with Chrysler, GM, and Ford, and with Northern Telecom and de Havilland. Sometimes, especially during negotiations when we were booked up in hotels for weeks at a time, or when flying without enough sleep in winter through turbulence and into territory unfamiliar to me, like Gander, Newfoundland, the job pushed me almost beyond endurance. I tried to keep my personal problems in the back of my mind and hide my panic attacks, but was not always successful. When my luggage – including my campaign files – was lost on a flight from Toronto to Gander, I fell apart. I had no clean clothes to wear, or even a toothbrush because the shops were all closed when I arrived. But those were minor inconveniences compared to my greatest fear, that the files would end up in the wrong hands. Other CAW staff members staying at the Gander Hotel, where our meetings were taking place, didn't seem that worried about my plight. Seasoned travellers, they knew that bags got lost all the time. But I was swept up by paranoia. I couldn't sleep and was afraid to leave my hotel room. Fortunately, one small act of kindness – for sometimes that is all it takes – eased me out of that bad spell. Buzz gave me a fresh sweatshirt to wear. My luggage, including the files, didn't appear until I was back in Toronto a week later. It was delivered, intact, to my doorstep.

Negotiations are the ritualization of class warfare. During the CAW negotiations I worked on, the service reps and other staff – research, legal, and communications people – specialists whom Bob called "the technicians," would move into a hotel with the negotiating team. It was the Sheraton Hotel in downtown Toronto for Chrysler, the Royal York for GM, and the Westbury for Ford. These incubators for testosterone brought out the worst and best in people, as the company and the union hammered out agreements that covered everything from wages and benefits to safety equipment, pensions, health plans, child care, and substance abuse. It was my job to liaise with the pack of journalists who camped outside the rooms for news – organizing the press conferences if needed, answering questions as best I could, monitoring the daily media coverage or issuing releases if clarification was needed. The union and the company would each have a bargaining agenda and set of principles, shopping lists of sorts. They would exchange these as starting points. The sides would listen to each other. Then the union negotiating committee would take the proposals away to examine them, clause by clause, complete with calculators and sharp shouting matches. The loud voices and the cursing, the cigars and cigarettes, though completely unnecessary, were part of a ritual that had been started who knows when and by who knows whom.

Was the offer good enough? Could we do better? When the team reached an agreement, the union would phone the company room and call everyone back to the table to either accept or reject the offer, piece by piece. All notions of time changed as days turned into nights and into days again. All sense of the outside world disappeared at the centre of this intense, embattled universe of wits and bravado. That was the easy part, for I got to work with the members of the negotiating teams – people like Charlie Stock from Northern Telecom, and expert servicing staff reps like Pat Clancy, Ron Pellerin, Ron Dickson, and Jim Kennedy. I also met good journalists and enjoyed the banter and the theatrics built into the process. John McGrath from the CBC and Jennifer Lanthier from *The Financial Post* are the two I remember most fondly as we all played our respective parts in the chaotic ritual of modern class warfare.

The hard part of my job began when the clock moved towards a midnight strike deadline. Loaded down with files, notes, and my laptop computer, I would jump into a taxi and head to Brampton and the printers to produce a ratification brochure. This was before modems. Most of the small bargaining items would be in place by this point, but the big items, often the monetary ones and most contentious, would still be outstanding. While I was in the back seat of the taxi the two sides at the hotel would still be at it, right down to the last second. If the union decided to accept the agreement, I had one night and a day to write and produce the ratification brochure that would highlight the package that the negotiating team would have to present to the members for approval. While writing I would keep in contact with Peggy and the others at the hotel by fax and telephone, adding items and changing language as we "got down to the short strokes." With two typesetters and a layout person, we would put the constantly changing package together. It wouldn't be finished until I had received the message from Bob, in which he would explain why he was endorsing the agreement. All the i's would have to be dotted and the t's crossed before the brochure was handed over to the printers, who were usually pacing the floor of the plant outside the composing room, waiting for the pages. Once printed, the four-page brochure would be bundled and shipped directly to the locals. Dizzy from lack of sleep I would return to my house for a few hours' rest before heading out to cover the meeting where the team would present the offer. Sometimes it would be a formality by this point, and the offer would sail through without much debate. Sometimes all hell would break loose, and the leadership would have to fight for its political life.

When I joined the CAW staff, Ron Kaplansky, a graphic designer who had designed the CAW's new publications and logos after the break from the UAW, and who knew the union culture well, gave me some survival advice: "Smile sweetly, and wear a frilly dress with army boots." There were only a handful of women reps on staff when I joined. The CAW was a tough environment for a woman, especially a mother. But, to be fair, it was tough for men too. Like most private-sector unions the CAW is structured along military lines. While the chain of command is clear, the protocols that support it are not. At least they weren't to me. Since there was nothing soft and fuzzy about how the CAW did things – no place for staffers like me in what we now call the "process" – I had some pretty rude awakenings. It was quietly acknowledged among staff that there were two teams in the union – the A-Team and the B-Team. Nobody wanted to be on the B-Team, but many of us were, and competition for "White's ear," the envied spot, was hot. This jockeying rite was common to all organizational and political life, but it surprised me that it took place in a labour movement culture. I thought that as brothers and sisters, we were supposed to operate as a case of "from each according to their ability, to each according to their need."

At the CAW I saw a lot of people under stress – the adrenalin rushes, the fatigue, the fears of failure, of letting the side down. I also saw the members exhilarated by the victories, like when the Fishermen, Food and Allied Workers succeeded in becoming a part of the union. I saw members devastated by losses, like the Michelin Tire organizing drive in Atlantic Canada and the plant closures that were being announced weekly. By the time I left the CAW I could identify team players and prima donnas, recognize courage and cowardice. I also learned something really significant, that none of these qualities are absolute. Cowards one day could be courageous the next. When I was doing research for stories for the union's magazine, I heard about the families and childhoods of the working-class people who were my co-workers and members of the union. I learned about the history of the union – the bloody strike at United Aircraft, the 1945 Windsor strike, the fight for the right to refuse unsafe work. I learned about its heroes, like the great Walter Reuther, the visionary UAW president who died in a plane crash in April 1970, years before the formation of the Canadian Union.

My father used to cite the famous line by the Scottish poet Robbie Burns, "*O wad some Pow'r the giftie gie us / To see oursels as others see us!*" One of my rudest awakenings was the discovery that I was seen by some in the organization to be not particularly well-suited to the job. I was perceived to be the sensitive artist-type, and some in the union were not yet ready to accommodate that type. Sam, the academic and also an "outsider" in that he had not come up through the union's ranks, told me not to worry about it. "If they can come to accept an absent-minded professor like me," he said, "they'll come to accept an artist too." Maybe the first step, however, was to be accepted as a working mother. Union culture, especially in the still male-dominated private sector like the CAW, was brutal, and I was not well cut out to be a man.

When I was producing a poster for the union's annual United Way campaign, I asked Owen Sound photographer Wally Watterson to get a photo of the children who were attending one of the union's family education programs. Although I asked for a shot of two children running a three-legged race, I wanted the image to represent the different ways in which we are all tied to each other, indicating that an injury to one is an injury to all. As a mother, I was tied to Grayson, and although I could see that he was stumbling, and about to fall, I didn't have the wherewithal to slow down, much less stop running. The caw was committed to antiracism and to the family and community. Politics is supposed to be the art of the possible. But try as I might, I couldn't figure out how to convey and integrate the personal with the union work, my feminism, my art, and my socialism. An Anne Sexton poem, "The Falling Dolls," describes the horror of watching thousands of dolls falling from the sky, and the help-lessness of being on the ground below trying to catch them. I felt like that.

> I hold open my arms
> and catch
> one,
> two, three ... ten in all,
> running back and forth like a badminton player,
> catching the dolls, the babies I practice upon, but others crack
> on the roof
> and I dream awake, I dream of falling dolls
> who need cribs and blankets and pyjamas
> with real feet in them.
> Why is there no mother?
> Why are all these dolls falling from the sky?
> Was there a father?
> Or have the planets cut holes in their nets
> and let our children out,
> or are we the dolls themselves,
> born but never fed?

In 1987 the dolls were falling, not just at home but everywhere as the recession drew nearer and nearer to everyone's doorstep. Though I could disengage emotionally from some of the union work, do it on a kind of technical automatic pilot, most of it couldn't be done that way. In May 1989 the Freuhauf plant in Mississauga in southern Ontario was closed down. The Freuhauf closure did not happen overnight, nor was it an isolated event in those days of plant shutdowns. The prosperity of North America's postwar boom, the promise that had brought my family to Canada, was over. The economy was in a nosedive. Free trade had won. Corporations were restructuring at breakneck speed. Entire operations were being moved to the United States or Mexico, where labour costs were cheap, environmental standards lax, labour legislation weak, and profit margins high. Or companies were downsizing.

Today restructuring and downsizing are so commonplace that we can forget that in the late '80s it was all shocking and new. Trailmobile bought Freuhauf in Mississauga and was moving production to Ingersoll and Brantford. Freuhauf, a well-known name in trailer and tank manufacturing, was CAW Local 252's oldest unit. A job at Freuhauf was supposed to be a good job, and a job for life. In its heyday the plant had supported a working population of nearly seven hundred. The layoffs started right away and a committee was hastily struck to assist displaced workers. A giant "for lease" sign was erected outside the plant and the equipment was auctioned off.

When I visited the plant on the morning of its last day with photographer David Hartman, it looked like a bomb site. The once beautiful lawns surrounding the building had been invaded by dandelions, which had gone to seed. Inside, the few remaining workers, those with the highest seniority, were dazed, sweeping up the scraps of their livelihoods with push brooms. One man was disassembling the last crane.

We found the former plant chairperson, David Marcus, huddled with three other men in the union office. The conversation was riddled with anger and bitterness. Fatigued, defeated, and betrayed, the men blamed themselves for not having answers to questions about pensions and what was then called unemployment insurance that the panicked members had thrown at them. The company had not given them the information. They blamed the union for not handling the situation better. They blamed the free-trade deal. One man blamed real-estate speculators, who were cleaning up in the wake of the closure.

Marcus told me that every two weeks since the announcement had been made, he had watched another group of workers leave in shock. Some people broke down completely. They were mostly middle-aged, too young to retire but too old to get hired. For Marcus, it was more than a job he was losing. As a CAW delegate to the Labour Council of Metropolitan Toronto and York Region, and an outspoken human rights activist, without the job, he had no union.

The social safety net became more than a concept for me that day. If workers were dealing with stress levels like the ones I witnessed, then family support services, like those provided by Huntley Youth Services, were needed. It became clear that if so many people were losing jobs, the unemployment insurance program couldn't be cut. If the women at Freuhauf were to be retrained, more child care was needed. If working-class families were going to have the strength to deal with the financial pressures, the public health system was as important as ever. If workers were losing their homes, more affordable housing was essential.

It's easy to buy into the myth that unions are big and powerful, but I understood then why unions had to work in harmony with others in the social movement. Years ago when the OFL had started building links with Action Daycare and others in the child-care community, I had thought the big strong unions were doing the day-care community a favour. I now saw the interdependence. The Freuhauf closure was the first time I really felt the limits and fragility of union power, and why unions had fought so hard over the years to put the social safety net in place. When there is no job, there is no union. The social safety net was put in place following the Great Depression of the 1930s. It was good to know it was there during the postwar years of prosperity, and it was even more necessary as we moved into the 1990s. Young people were beginning to lose hope in the future. Mine was not the only troubled family. Huntley

Youth Services was taxed to the limit and could not keep up with the demand for its services.

One weekend I suggested to Grayson that we take off, just the two of us, and drive to Niagara Falls. We had always enjoyed car trips, so I was pleased when he agreed to go with me to Niagara Falls. As usual, we brought music tapes to play. That weekend Grayson brought tapes of some of the angry new music coming out of the disenchanted youth culture in Margaret Thatcher's Britain. One of the tapes was by a band called Screwdriver, which I realized was capitalizing on the poverty and desperation in that country to inflame race hatred. He had other music too, which he explained was called "Oi," that was not racist, but angrily expressed a hard-edged class consciousness. With free trade and the Brian Mulroney Tories, Canada was just beginning to move into its Thatcherism, but the culture she had created among the poor had already travelled the ocean and was influencing the values of some young Canadians.

By dusk we were driving through the Niagara Falls industrial back streets, past its closed factories and abandoned yards. He played "Dirty Old Town" by the Pogues. I thought of Glasgow. I played Bruce Springsteen's "My Hometown." In the United States, under Ronald Reagan, the industrial jobs were indeed going and "they weren't coming back."

We stayed at the Holiday Inn, where Grayson spent most of the time in front of the video game screens, stubbornly behind the line he had drawn between us. Soon after that trip, in 1988, Grayson moved out of the house. When I pleaded with him, warning him about the dangers of the street, straining to keep my voice light, all he said was, "I don't need your fuckin' sympathy, Mom." I didn't know where he was going.

A big part of my CAW job involved shovelling the snowbanks of paper that accumulated on my desk each morning. Most of it went into the waste basket, and some of it to files. Weeks after Grayson disappeared I picked up a fax of a newspaper story and picture. The photo was of a gang of bald boys in bomber jackets and army boots. It had been sent to me by Adam Czerechowicz, whom I hadn't heard from in several years. The headline said, "The Young Face of Racism in Canada." I didn't get it at first. Then I saw a quote from Grayson, expounding on the merits of white power and the danger of interracial marriage. The article said that the group of skinheads held weekly Saturday morning meetings at a restaurant in the Rosedale section of Toronto. It didn't name the restaurant, but it indicated that the meetings were organized by Don Andrews, a high-profile rightwinger and racist whom I had first heard about in my student days at the University of Toronto.

On the following Saturday morning, after several sleepless nights, I drove with D'Arcy to every restaurant in the Rosedale area. At each place D'Arcy would pull the car up on the curb while I ran in to look for Grayson. After half a dozen tries, through a window I spotted a group of earnest young men and women sitting in booths at Druxy's Deli on Yonge Street. When I went into the restaurant the youngsters and the adults with them rose to their feet and slowly backed away from me. I spotted Grayson and signalled him to come and talk to me. I kept my voice low and tried to maintain my composure, but I was shaking. I asked him to come home. Not that moment, but, please, by supper time. D'Arcy and I drove back to the house, and I spent the rest of the day watching the clock, bitting my nails and chain smoking.

He came, and we talked. He told me I had scared the life out of his buddies that morning. They thought I had a gun. That night we began the negotiating session of my lifetime, and our starting positions were miles apart. A few weeks later I received a call from Grayson's friend Samantha telling me Grayson had been arrested in a police raid, along with several others, and charged with assault. He was being held at the Western Detention Centre.

I went to the detention centre and spoke to Grayson through the glass in a prison visiting room. I posted bail, and he was released. Not long after he was picked up again and charged with breaking and entering a shoe store on Queen Street. As had been the case in the first incident, the charges were dropped. The police had no evidence. With street violence on the rise and racial tensions mounting in Toronto, the police were clamping down. Harassment was one of the methods they used. Innocent or not, boys who dressed in the way Grayson did at the time – in bomber jackets and Doc Marten boots, with shaved heads – were prime targets. I was almost ready to give up. The streets were dangerous, his friends were dangerous, his ideas were dangerous, but he didn't have the sense to come home. He refused to go to school. He wasn't working. He was drinking too much, though he swore he didn't do drugs; his gang was against drugs. But they weren't averse to the street fights that their outfits invited.

My friends on the left were shocked and upset and perplexed by Grayson's right-wing ideas, and many of them quietly turned away from us. During this time I took up the ritual of driving along Queen Street, in order to stop my car in front of the Catholic church near Sherbourne, across from the Good Shepherd Mission. In front of that church is a statue of the pietà, the mother of Christ holding the broken and lifeless body of her crucified son. It was there that I said my prayer for all of us – those who were already on the street, and the army of poor that I knew by then would be coming soon – and I prayed for myself. For being born poor. For making mistakes. For making decisions without knowing why, then changing my mind. For wanting to do my own thing. For falling in love with the wrong people for the wrong reasons. For getting drunk to ease the pain. And for never learning to fight properly. One day, pulling away from Queen and Sherbourne I found a kind of answer to my prayers. Out loud I said the words: "Screw all this guilt."

Later, opening the mail on my desk I came across a book from Covenant House, a home for street kids. The title was *Sometimes God Has a Child's Face*. After reading the little book from cover to cover, I didn't feel guilty. I felt determined. Grayson was not going to be abandoned to the streets. As much as I despised his ideas and his attitudes, I accepted that it was my responsibility to bring him home. Roaming the streets was bad enough. Roaming the streets with his ideas was even worse. My son belonged with me, not with the police or in a morgue.

Someone had suggested Huntley Youth Services for family coun-
selling. The organization had a staff counsellor who specialized in the
Toronto gang scene. I kept hearing about tough love, the parenting philosophy that recommends changing the locks at home and cutting the little
bastards off completely. I couldn't buy that. I did some one-to-one talking
with the Huntley Street counsellor and tried to get Grayson involved in it
too, with some success, but we still seemed to be going nowhere fast. So I
helped organize weekly meetings for other mothers whose children were
connected to gangs. For several summer months the most tired-looking
group of mothers I had ever seen offered each other support and hope. We
represented all classes and ethnic and racial groups, drawn together
because each of us was either afraid for, or afraid of, our children. The stories I heard from the terrified mothers of young neo-nazis, Satan worship-
pers, and, in one case, an animal torturer, were heartbreaking.

When a television journalist working on a documentary about street
gangs heard about our meetings she asked for permission to sit in and listen. We were all vulnerable and probably should have been protected from
her intrusion by the Huntley Street professional staff, but when she asked
if she could interview a few of us, and maybe our children, without thinking it through some of us agreed to do it. I even talked Grayson into participating. I thought it might do some good. Now, I have made some tough
judgement calls in my time, but I still can't tell if this was the worst or the
best decision I ever made. I had taught Grayson to look both ways before
crossing the street, but by encouraging him to speak the truth about who
he was and what he was thinking, I threw him right under the wheels of
the media. The journalist got her story. It aired. I was presented as a concerned and overwrought mother; Grayson came across as a charming,
articulate, fifteen-year-old right-winger and street fighter.

I suppose it was an accurate depiction of the image he wished to project in the summer when the show was filmed, but by the time the show
aired in December he had already changed his lifestyle. He had left Toronto and the gang scene and found a factory job in a new town, where he set

up house with Samantha. He returned to school. Bit by bit he started to put a new life together. But when the program aired again when he was seventeen, then again when he was eighteen, I realized that with my blessing, television had frozen him in time. Each time the show aired, we heard about it. His bosses saw the show, his teachers saw the show. His impressionable young classmates, who looked up to him because he was older, saw the show, too. It became nearly impossible for Grayson to escape from the racism and violence in his past. Because of his reputation he was regularly challenged to fight. But still, if I had not agreed to do the interviews for the documentary, Grayson might have gone along unchallenged. The show made him think about and rethink his ideas, which gradually, on his own, he found harder and harder to defend.

I don't know how I would have reacted if someone had documented me when I was an inexperienced young Trotskyist sympathizer calling for a dictatorship of the proletariat, or an inexperienced young feminist talking earnestly about smashing monogamy. On the other hand, had I not been a young Trotskyist sympathizer or a socialist feminist who had grown and changed and learned from my experience, I might not have had the empathy to hold onto my child as he passed through his own rebellion.

As Grayson found his feet we gradually and tentatively approached the line that had been drawn between us. During long and often heated conversations about the world and how we each saw it, I learned that he had once interpreted my ideas about racial and gender equality, and the discussions about "white men in suits," as meaning I hated white men. We talked about economic inequality and this, in turn, led to conversations about what we thought it meant to be proud of our own roots and culture, even though we weren't born with silver spoons in our mouths.

We agreed that human dignity, the abuse of power, and the right of everyone to grow in the best traditions of their own cultures were top issues. We couldn't possibly do this without encouraging diversity. The political problem is to find ways to create the conditions in which these things can happen. From what had looked like extreme opposite positions,

13

Good Medicine, and a Gift of Life

The more I talked to men as well as women, the more it seemed
that inner feelings of incompleteness, emptiness, self-doubt,
and self-hatred were the same, no matter who experienced
them, and even if they were expressed in culturally opposite
ways. I don't mean to gloss over the difficulties of equalizing
power, even where there is the will to do so: to the overvalued
and defensive, the urge to control and dominate others may be
as organic as a mollusk's shell; and to the undervalued and
resentful, the power to destroy the self (and others who resemble
the self) may be the only power there is. But at both extremes —
as well as in more subtle areas between, where most of us
struggle every day — people seemed to stop punishing others or
themselves only when they gained some faith in their own unique,
intrinsic worth.

Gloria Steinem, *Revolution from Within:*
A Book of Self-Esteem (1992)

PHILOSOPHER JAMES HILLMAN has an exercise he encourages his readers to do, as a simple way of demonstrating a point about perspective.

Think about looking out your home's window. In daylight you might see neighbours leaving their homes, putting out their garbage, heading off to work, or children going off to school, their mittens trailing behind them like kite tails. You can probably see the sky and make predictions about the weather. Perhaps there's a tree you can watch as the seasons change, like the magnolia that for one dramatic and breathtaking week each spring bursts into flower outside my window. When night falls, if the lights in the room are off, and the moon is bright, you can still see out the window. But the moment you hit the light switch, all you will be able to see in that same window is your own reflection and a reflection of the room you stand in.

Being able to recognize myself – to know myself – has always been important to me, but it has never been enough. For I live in a world that is much bigger than I am, and I have responsibilities in a large and diverse human community. The problem is, when you get out into that world it becomes not only possible but convenient to neglect the personal or spiritual housework that also has to be done. As I learned, I couldn't get away with this basic approach forever.

In 1989 D'Arcy and I finally turned the light on inside our relationship, and neither of us much liked what we saw. The flash point came one evening at Harbourfront's Power Plant Gallery, where we had gone to look at an exhibition of work by the controversial young painter Attila Richard Lucas. Grayson and I were still engaged in our negotiations, and I was interested to see what the artist had to say about the skinhead culture he was representing in his paintings. The evidence around us was that a worsening economy was fuelling skinhead culture and racism. The neo-Nazi Nationalist Party of Canada was getting a lot of media exposure with its exploitation of youth anger and rebellion. A right-wing weekend gathering had recently taken place in Minden, Ontario, complete with a cross-burning. At the gallery I expected to find a curator's statement that would present Lucas's work in this context. That was not the case.

The paintings of heroic, naked, and tattooed boys in jackboots were technically good, rendered powerfully in layers of paint, roofing tar, and gold leaf. Stylistically they reminded me of giant-scale versions of the beautiful holy cards I used to press into my prayer book as a child – classic religious images and icons. But the nuns and priests who gave me these cards knew, even if I didn't, that the cards served an ideological mission – the propagation of the Catholic faith. Lucas appeared to be fascinated with fascism. There was little ambiguity in his startling images.

As I looked at the art, the comments I heard around me made me feel that the viewers were so fascinated with Lucas's sense of style that they were ignoring the subject at the heart of the art. It seemed to me that a variant of the nasty, racist wars of the twentieth century was marching again, unchecked, into fashionable art galleries, to be trivialized as dinner-table conversation about paint and technique. I became overwhelmed by a sense of danger. Once again I was being profoundly and personally activated by a work of art.

Right then and there, as a handful of people in the gallery gathered around curiously and nervously, I went into a rant about the need for art galleries to take responsibility for work they exhibited. To shut me up, a nervous gallery worker shoved the guest book in front of me and invited me to write down my comments. When D'Arcy gently attempted to usher me out of the room, I pushed him away. I wasn't ready to be polite.

Later, outside, sitting on a bench facing the lake, I tried to cool down. My acute reaction to the work was no doubt triggered by my lifetime fear of Nazism and my all-too-recent wrestling match with Grayson and his skinhead friends. I have never understood how ordinary, decent people let the Holocaust happen. Those who have studied evil conclude that all it takes for evil to triumph is for honest people do nothing. In her galvanizing personal account of the Serbo-Croatian war, *The Balkan Express: Fragments from the Other Side of the War*, Croatian journalist Slovenka Drakulic talks frankly about her own ability to deny the horror of what was happening in her country, her own inability to accept the truth of the war, even when the war zone was a hundred, then twenty, miles from her own doorstep. Even though Drakulic saw thousands of refugees coming from the battlefronts to seek safety in her city – even though she heard the stories of brutality, rape and ethnic cleansing, she still managed to separate herself from their experience. Reflecting on this phenomenon, Drakulic mentions a man interviewed for the Holocaust film *Shoah*. When asked what it had been like to farm so near the barbed wire and screams of the Treblinka Nazi concentration camp, the man said that at first he found it unbearable and then he got used to it.

D'Arcy joined me for a moment and then left. Not long after I went to my car and drove home, as quickly as I could. I would pack my suitcase and get out of our house. I had to leave. But D'Arcy beat me to it. We met on the doorstep, and he already had a suitcase in his hand. I could imagine the spirit of my mother, shaking her finger at me sadly, as she always did when one of my relationships ended. "I told you so," she was saying. "You should have married Martin Quinn."

Depending on whom I was talking to, I chose one of two dozen ways of explaining the breakup. D'Arcy was too committed to his work. Our class differences were too great. I had to make a choice between Grayson and D'Arcy. I was too volatile for D'Arcy. He was too busy for me. My spirit humanism clashed with his economic materialism. I could have said that our relationship died when the skinheads marched into our home. I could have said that our love was killed by art in the Power Plant Gallery. Each and all of these were true to some extent. But relationships form for mysterious reasons, and they break up for mysterious reasons too. The good thing about the timing was that it finally gave me the time and the space I needed to confront myself. In that time and space I found myself doing something about my drinking habits.

Before the breakup I had learned about the CAW's substance abuse program from my co-worker Jim Kennedy when he dropped into my office one day for some communications assistance. He wanted a new sign to advertise the fellowship room at an upcoming CAW Council meeting. He talked to me about some ideas he had for promoting the work of the union's growing network of local union substance-abuse representatives. Jim told me the goals of the CAW's program were to make substance abuse a bargaining table issue, to educate members about the dangers of addic-

tion, and to work to secure treatment resources. He thought a video might
be a useful tool. Realizing that anyone with a substance-abuse problem
would not particularly want to see a half-hour lecture on drugs and alcohol, I suggested that we make a short music video that could be plugged,
like an ad, into any of the union's educational programs. We would produce an accompanying brochure that interested members could read in
private.

We called the new campaign "Recovery," and as I drafted a CAW statement of principles, I took a first giant step towards my own sobriety, away
from the alcohol that had been an unhappy part of my family's history for
generations, which had killed both my grandfathers, caused my grandmothers and my mother endless worry, and in the here and now was
threatening to capture Grayson – for heavy drinking was a big part of
skinhead life. I decided I could try to tackle a soul-destroying and often
violent cycle that loomed as large as childhood poverty and powerlessness
in my consciousness. "Alcohol and drugs can be walls that keep us from
seeing our own personal worth," I wrote for the Recovery brochure. "Our
recovery program is build on a concept of self-worth."

> A strong sense of self-worth is something history has denied
> workers. The CAW has fought for dignity in the workplace, for
> better wages and working conditions. The Recovery program
> expands these concerns because we believe our responsibility
> doesn't end at the plant gate. . . . A successful Recovery pro-
> gram will only happen when we live up to our belief that an
> injury to one is an injury to all of us. As long as one brother or
> sister is neglected, the full potential for our union is unrealized.

We also applied successfully to the Ontario Arts Council for funding from
what was then a new Artists in the Workplace program. We used the grant
to hire poet Phil Hall to work with the substance-abuse committee in
Windsor. Phil would lead a series of creative writing workshops with

members who wanted to write about their own struggles with substance abuse, and the union would publish their work in a collection we eventually called *Liquid Lunch*. Although the CAW Recovery program included, but was not limited to, the Alcoholics Anonymous model, we respected the anonymity of the writers when we published their work. Several pieces that came out of these workshops were also published in the Recovery brochure, including the following poem.

The Rage Gone

Especially in the morning,
when the long day stretches infinitely in your mind,
there is an allure about this amber substance,
a suggestion of comfort, felicity, escape;
and then that crucial moment
when your nose stops running, your eyes dry,
and with the mask firmly in place
you look forward to the sky for signs.

Later,
weary of pretense,
when you've discovered something else,
maturity maybe, but high on yourself,
the rage gone,
you walk the streets unafraid,
clear eyes searching for contact,
once again, with the human family.

The project gave me the opportunity to call Lorraine Segato. I had not worked with her since we made the film *Worth Every Minute*, with Pat Schulz. By then Lorraine was a Juno award-winning musician with her band The Parachute Club and one of English-speaking Canada's most politically active artists. She agreed immediately to work with us. As a musician in an industry also plagued with substance-abuse problems, she liked the idea that the CAW Recovery program was built on the concept of collective self-esteem and appreciated that she was not being asked to write yet another simple "just say no" anti-drug song. I arranged for her to meet with the chairperson of the union's substance abuse committee, who in turn introduced Lorraine to his committee members and other workers at the Ford plant in Oakville, Ontario. She listened to their personal stories and, based on them, she went to work with her songwriting colleague Dave Gray. They drafted the lyrics and Lorraine outlined a script for what became the *Good Medicine* music video. It dramatized one man's battle with booze and cocaine. She showed drafts of her work to the members and incorporated their comments into her rewrites.

To play the troubled CAW member we hired film and television actor David Nerman, and to play his spouse, Rebecca Jenkins. We shot the workplace scenes at the giant Boeing/ de Havilland plant, with Local 252 members performing as extras. The local's president, Jerry Dias, agreed to make a cameo appearance as a bartender. When the video was finished, it aired regularly on Much Music television. We hoped the union's openness about substance abuse would make it easier for members to get assistance if they needed it.

The *Good Medicine* project had just wrapped up when the Harbourfront incident took place. Then, one evening, I was sitting in my favourite chair with my feet up and a glass of scotch in my hand, beginning to survey the house and think about the changes I would have to make now that D'Arcy was gone. I was relatively content. The project had gone well. Grayson was in better shape – controlling his drinking and having made a decision to leave Toronto and go back to school. Music was playing. When Grayson and Samantha arrived that night for a visit, Samantha took one look at me and said, "Poor Catherine, sitting home on a Friday night, drinking alone." I tried to deny it, but it was true. I immediately saw what could happen to me if I wasn't careful. Alcohol had long ago lost its power to make me feel happy. I knew, in fact, it had the opposite effect on me, and I realized I was going to need a clear head to work my way through the next few months. To this day I bless Samantha's heart for carrying the message to me.

But there would be one more sobering experience before I quit drinking completely – the Montreal Massacre. In December 1989, fourteen women students were shot in cold blood by a single gunman. The killer separated them out from the men in their classroom, called them feminists, and shot them. Women all across the country were in shock. We were all afraid. When the union asked me to draft a public statement, I realized as I was writing it that it was time for me to recommit myself to the women's struggle. Yes, we had come a long way, but we still had a long way to go. All around me I heard people arguing about whether the massacre was a political act or a purely personal tragedy. It was both. It seemed to me that if a gunman walked into the middle of a bargaining session, asked the union negotiators to leave, called the others a "bunch of rotten capitalists," and then executed them, this old separation of the political from the personal would certainly not have come into play.

I realized I was still living in a man's world – a world blind to the depth of its sexism, that "virulent social disease" that thrives through behaviour, language, and political and business policy, among other things. As long as women stay "in their place" – as mothers, homemakers, nurses, or darners of socks – they get a traditional modicum of acknowledgement and honour. (The greeting card companies have given us "Mother's Day," after all.) When women try to do something about institutionalized oppression, trouble starts.

I also realized that I couldn't try to change the world if I was not willing to change myself. The women of Alcoholics Anonymous told me that drinking problems had nothing to do with alcohol. Alcoholism is a disease of the spirit. It is about fear of the future and shame about the past. They helped me to practise living in the present by facing up to the truth about my past and by trying to make amends for mistakes I had made, wherever possible. Besides that, they told me, forget about the past and stop worrying about the future. Live one day at a time. They said that if I did this without clouding my mind with drink, I would find that the past and future, those two weighty eternities, would stop controlling my life.

I decided to trust them. Although Alcoholics Anonymous was based on a strict Christian tradition, they said that I could think about God or a higher power in any way I wanted to. I chose to think that if there were a God, she was probably female. I chose to think of my religion as my socialism. The women made no attempt to try and make me believe things I couldn't believe. Keep it simple, they told me. Put first things first. And I did.

For nearly thirty years I had kept myself as far away from the institutional Catholic church as possible. Tentatively, however, I had recently begun to approach my granite notions about religion, as a sculptor approaches a slab of rock, in the hope that perhaps, inside the unforgiving mass, may lie a spirit I could identify and thus release.

That Christmas was my first sober Christmas in years. The house was empty and quiet compared to the bustle and activity of previous years, but I was learning to live comfortably with my own company. D'Arcy, Danielle, and Nyranne were gone. Katheryne Schulz, who usually spent Christmas with me, was in Nicaragua, doing volunteer work with community organizations. Grayson, happily, was planning on spending a few days with me. I put up a tree, placed a few gifts under it, and decorated the house in preparation for his visit.

A snowstorm Christmas eve transformed the night into a winter beauty. Grayson agreed to indulge me and accompany me to midnight mass at Holy Rosary Church. As we drove through the almost deserted streets, I thanked God we were together and safe. We had survived. I heard the words to all the usual Christmas carols at the church as though I were hearing them for the first time. Later, when Grayson and I exchanged gifts, I opened his present to me and found a small framed photograph of himself as a shy, young boy, cradling a puppy. On Christmas morning I dressed early and made my way to the Jesuit Centre for Social Faith and Justice at Pape and Queen. A friend, Deborah Barndt, who worked at the centre, had invited me there to share in a mass with a group of Salvadorean refugees who had just arrived in Canada from their war-torn country. From there Grayson and I made our way to Julie Davis's home, where we visited with a number of friends who had supported Grayson and me in various ways through all the ups and downs of the previous difficult years.

◇

Around Christmas of 1989 a spontaneous party broke out after a staff meeting at the CAW Family Education Centre in Port Elgin, Ontario. Craig Grant had his guitar with him and was playing tunes. Glen Myers had a great blues voice. It was well after midnight, but the bar was still open. People slowly gathered around and began making requests. Bob White and Buzz Hargrove were joined by a backup chorus and did a few respectable interpretations of Elvis Presley songs, "Hound Dog," "Heartbreak Hotel," and the like – with fancy footwork and moves. Bob did a show-stopping interpretation of the Sinatra song "My Way." When it was my turn I took the mike and belted out Patsy Cline's "Crazy," with all my heart. It had been years since I had sung in public. It had been even more years since I had done it when I was completely sober. Everybody knew the words and sang along. In that rare moment of down time at the CAW it was as if I were back in my grandmother's living room on a Sunday night. And I knew for sure, maybe for the first time in my life, that I wasn't crazy. I was just as strong in my own way as any of the guys, though in ways they may not ever know or recognize. (By then it didn't matter whether they knew it or not.)

I had come to realize that in political life, as in the theatre, and as in the women's and student movements, groups of people come together for short periods to work together on campaigns or productions. They are the army buddies, the friends you remember kindly and gratefully, but not the kind who are likely to drop in for Sunday dinner or remember your birthday. After the campaigns wind down or the last curtain falls, each of us moves on to a new job or a new production, where new alliances are made and the process begins once again. But, usually, each time this happens one or two or three of those people don't completely pass out of your life. At the CAW it was my co-workers Ron Dickson, Jim Kennedy and Bob Nickerson who stuck with me, guiding me and supporting me, and I will always be grateful to them.

In September 1990 I left the CAW and became one of the first to enlist when the Ontario New Democrats won their historic victory over David Peterson's Liberals. I wanted to work in the culture ministry, to help raise the issue of class bias and work towards legislation that would recognize the status of artists as workers. Though it seemed I had been in training for a moment like that all my life, I still wasn't ready for what I found. My time in the office of the Minister of Culture and Communications, and the later fight for labour law reform, showed me the difference between winning political office – which we had – and winning real political power, which it became clear to me we didn't have.

We were armed only with our odd collection of politics. Some of us in the Ministry of Culture and Communications came from labour, some were community activists, some were artists, some were NDP activists. We had sentimental, untried, and often competing visions of social justice. Until I worked in the minister's office, I had never considered Political work as real work. For some reason, I thought political workers were highly paid folks who sipped cocktails and chatted with smiling people, returning to their offices only late in the day to make phone calls, set up media appointments, smile a lot, and shake hands. The reality was that it was bloody hard work, drawing on all I knew and challenging all I held precious. It required immense co-ordination and flexibility, and carried with it the tremendous weights of accountability, responsibility, and scrutiny.

The recession had hit its mark. Thanks in no small measure to the Free Trade Agreement, we rocked in a wake of food banks, cutbacks, and plant closures. Unorganized workers were not just underpaid and often under-employed, but had no voice in the affairs of state. The growing legions of unemployed were filling in forms instead of working. The homeless were trying to keep warm. Women were demanding control over their bodies without forfeiting their souls. Environmentalists were losing their patience. Corporations were embracing free trade as a quick money scheme. Peace activists watched, in horror, as the superpowers fell into line in the Persian Gulf. Immigrants were learning the ropes without the language. Native people were facing the Canadian army. Hungry children were falling asleep in classrooms or in front of television sets. Young people were drunk or stoned and killing each other because their pain was too big. Churches were empty. And our social-democratic government was learning how difficult it is to govern with any sense of cohesion. We didn't even know how big the Ontario deficit was. Were we up to this task? Who were we anyway?

I suppose we were the "ordinary people" we used to read about in the NDP literature handed out by every self-respecting, left-leaning, type come election time. In the Culture minister's office there were no stars, no lawyers, no rich people. We had all, in our own ways, crawled across the cut glass of community service and anti-establishment cultural and political activism. After a month on the job it seemed like I had not slept properly, had not eaten properly, and wasn't sure of my footing. Like the others around me, it seemed I was having to make decisions too quickly for comfort. Despite all this, what we were trying to do still felt good.

At the Ministry of Culture and Communications, we had already agreed that we had to challenge existing definitions of art, culture, and communications. We had to try to demystify art and expand the confining, Eurocentric definition of culture. No comprehensive NDP cultural policy yet existed, nor any comprehensive labour policy, for that matter. That meant we had to tackle concepts like access, inclusion, cultural affirmative action, communications, marketing, public education, and distribution. If we were to convince the NDP cabinet that culture needed a bigger share of the provincial budget, we would have to show taxpayers that culture mattered. I saw it as an issue of national defence against the culture and values of our intrusive neighbour to the south.

Instead of wielding power, though, a group of us soon found we were picking over bone-dry budgets. Like the others on staff, including Adrianna Tetley, who had come from the OFL, and Jonathan Forbes, who had come from Toronto's Development Education Centre, I sometimes worked fifteen-hour days and seven-day weeks trying to make it work. First of all I had to learn that making government is not a linear task, with a set of steps to accomplish, a deadline to meet, and a product at the end. In the government of those years, the systems were big and rusty. Access was difficult. And we didn't control the corporations or the money markets that still called the shots.

It seemed that our phones never stopped ringing. Everybody wanted something, and not always concrete things like money. That might have been easier. Then we could have asked the callers for their names, their addresses, how much they wanted, and what they wanted it for. When people phoned the minister's office, more often than not all they wanted was the right to inform and be informed. They wanted recognition. There was always a line-up of requests for the minister's presence at public events, letters of greeting, and letters of understanding. There were countless requests for private meetings, a chance to shake hands, and, even if it was for just twenty minutes, a chance to speak "the truth" to someone in power. To meet the demand for recognition, the minister would have had to be cut into a hundred pieces a day.

The job of government is to circulate all these demands, so that a civil service, as big as a people's army, can meet as many of them as possible. As a working-class woman, I knew the importance of recognition, and as a worker in this new government I didn't want to perpetuate a culture of invisibility. So, like the others around me, I exhausted myself trying to deal with all the demands. We fought for access for as many people as possible to the systems of government, because we believed that a people can get what they need with good socialist leadership, with steadfast principles of justice, and the spirit and art of negotiation.

I knew by observing the Big Three negotiations with the CAW that agreements can be reached in which everyone wins. Given the chance, people can decide among themselves how to get what they need. Most people are not greedy, and I don't think people expected or wanted the new government to live their lives for them. People wanted a government that would listen to problems, treat new issues seriously, be unafraid of controversy, and find ways to shepherd urgencies through complex mazes of government.

We had a number of disappointments. When we made the decision not to fund the multimillion dollar ballet and opera house (after all, we were in a recession), we heard formally only from those who opposed our decision. Our friends, those who supported the move, didn't say so publicly. The ballet/opera house decision was our first face-off with the corporate community. It was also the first face we showed to the arts community, which was expecting and deserved so much from us. Many took it as a sign that we were against the arts. Those of us in the minister's office had tried to convince the NDP cabinet that we should announce our intentions to increase the funding to the Ontario Arts Council by twenty-five per cent at the same time as the ballet/opera house decision. But we were not given the go-ahead to do that. That denial was our first encounter with the slow cabinet process that all decisions had to go through.

We also experienced many small victories and encouragements. We funded community radio stations and kept community information centres open. We started to draft status of the artist legislation, to give artists the same rights as other workers. We met with hundreds of people and received lots of good ideas and advice. We became more familiar with cultural activities outside Toronto. When the Harbourfront coalition sprung into being in response to threatened federal cuts to cultural funding, it was like seeing the first crocus of spring.

◇

I will always be fascinated by the things that time allows us to throw away, and the things it makes us keep, like a photograph of a young Jesuit I carried in my wallet for many years. I met him in Muskoka in the summer of 1967 when I worked as a chambermaid at Gryphon Lodge. On the back of the photo he scribbled a note, telling me that I would meet many different people in my lifetime and that each of them would have a message for me. He told me to regard each of them, and the things they would teach me, as sacred. *This was advice I had not always heeded.*

One night in December 1990, late in the evening, my telephone rang. Katheryne Schulz was with me and picked up the phone. She knew I was tired and wasn't feeling like talking to anyone that late at night. She put her hand over the receiver and whispered, "It's a guy called Martin Quinn. He says it's important." I had not talked to Martin in over twenty-five years. I took the call. He had got my phone number from my brother, Robert, he said, and he was at the Toronto Airport, on his way to a horticultural meeting in Chicago. He wondered if I would have dinner with him on Friday evening when he returned. As we talked I found out his marriage had ended and that he needed a friend to talk to about it. After all these years he still regarded me as a friend. I said, yes, of course I'll see you.

When I told Grayson about the call he warned me that he wanted to meet anyone I was even thinking about dating. "Promise me you won't get involved with anyone, unless it's someone I can sit down and talk to, and someone who can throw a ball." I assured him that I was not looking for a new husband – it was the last thing on my mind – but that I would keep his advice in mind.

The evening spent with Martin couldn't have come at a better time. When I looked at him, and talked to him, I saw and heard a long-lost friend. He had greenhouses in the country and made plants grow. He was interested in politics, but could talk about other things. He was kind, soft-spoken, and interested in resuming our friendship. We continued seeing each other over the following year or two. We filled in the blanks of the thirty years we had been apart. He'd gone thataway. I'd gone thisaway, and we had finally met back at the ranch. We grew more and more attached to each other's company – and I became more and more interested in life as he was living it.

In March 1991 I took a two-week break from the Ontario government and rented a small cottage overlooking an ice-bound Lake Huron, just south of Kincardine. I settled in there with my computer and books to return to a few writing projects. I was living close to my sister Janis and brother Robert, and I realized how much I had missed a family life. I also realized how much I missed writing and doing my own work. I left the government job in June.

One day Martin suggested to me that I might find it easier to work at writing if I left Toronto and went to live with him in Strathroy, about a three-hour drive west of Toronto. Martin said Grayson could come to live there as well, and he promised to build a garden just for me and make sure I had a room of my own to write in. I was tempted, but resistant at first. I was worried, given past experience, about making a commitment, about making a new relationship work. I knew more than ever that I couldn't expect Martin, or anyone else, to solve my problems for me, make my life over. I had broken hearts, and my own heart had been broken often enough to leave me shy about full involvements. I was also not sure that Grayson would want to leave Toronto.

Then I decided, finally, to listen to my mother. I convinced myself that if Martin had gone to the trouble of searching me out, I would look upon his reappearance as one of life's mysteries, one of those rare surprise gifts of life that need not be questioned. Martin liked Grayson. He told me that he thought my son should be my first priority. Martin coached baseball, played hockey, activities that had been totally outside my life experience for years. We both enjoyed canoeing, cooking meals together, listening to old records. Martin had a big Bernese mountain dog called Woody who led us quietly on long country walks.

The Italian sociologist Francesco Alberoni noticed that people have a tendency to fall in love with people they believe to be better than themselves. Then they spend a great deal of energy trying to prove themselves deserving of their partner's love. It makes me think of the wisdom in the old folk song I used to sing with teenage passion and embryonic understanding: "*I leaned my back against an oak/ thinking it was a trusty tree/ but first it bent/ and then it broke/ just as my love proved false to me.*" It was not *the lover* but my *own love* that had proved false to me. I had never entered a relationship with anyone on a basis of rough equality: I always thought, whether consciously or unconsciously, that they were above me to a lesser or greater extent (though perhaps it didn't seem that way to them). Now, it seemed, an emerging sense of self-respect on my part was making possible a more balanced relationship. Or was this simply a case of the universe unfolding by chance?

The Quinn family had immigrated to western Ontario from Ireland and settled on a farm in the Kincardine area in the 1840s. Martin is what we tend to call a "family man," someone with a deep respect for women. The only son of a strong and determined mother, an English war bride, and a father who had left his home only once, to serve in the Canadian forces during the Second World War, Martin had grown up in a closely knit home in which the women worked alongside the men. His parents and four remarkable and hardworking sisters did whatever had to be done to keep the family florist and landscaping business going. I was told the Quinn children learned how to weed as soon as they could stand.

Martin introduced me to horticultural Latin, the language he could read and write with unqualified skill and grace. In his greenhouses he acquainted me with the poetry of artemesia, echinacea, eupatorium, angelica, lavundula, rudbeckia, and the dozens of other perennials and ornamental grasses he grew. A natural world, so different from the other worlds – industrial, urban – I had known, opened to me.

Martin also knew how to grow food and, amazingly, how to build a fire by rubbing sticks together. He understood first aid and how to set broken limbs, stop wounds from bleeding. He could fix cars. He was physically strong, and I liked watching him run and playing with the dog. Grayson would indeed have someone he could toss a ball around with. Martin was proud of having carried the Olympic torch on a bitterly cold day during the Canada Olympics. He understood weather, seasons, earth, and water – things I had never paid much attention to. Sometimes I would have an umbrella when it started to rain; more often I would not. I could drive a car, but if its engine stopped running, I was clueless.

When we drove the side roads of southern Ontario, Martin could point to a massive blue spruce tree that he had planted, one springtime, long ago, or to a mature forest that he and his father had planted, sapling by sapling. He knew who raised the barns, the ones that were still standing as well as the ones that were no more because of hurricanes with names and years he could recite. And he knew who lived in the farm houses we passed, places far back from the road, and who had lived there long before.

For my part, I enjoyed reading, and I had books and writing abilities that Martin appreciated. All his life he had experienced difficulties around those skills – the word-blindness, or dyslexia, that had made school a nightmare for him had never been diagnosed. I had a sense of organization and enjoyed the various tasks that went into making a home. I had something of tangible value to bring into the relationship, a sort of a dowry.

Neither of us was a luxury for the other; neither of us was perfect. We were both alone, and both of us wanted to be loved. More than that, both of us needed to love. Later, when Martin developed two new ornamental grasses – *miscanthus sinensis* – he asked me to help him name them. We both marvelled over the Lake Huron shoreline, and since the shimmering flowers of these grasses were golden and bronze, we called them Huron

Sunrise and Huron Sunset, a tribute to the place we had met as youngsters and to which we now decided we would return.

Years earlier I had reflected in one of my "anger poems" that "the female soul in chains is a bitch," and as I was making these post-romantic calculations I finally understood what I had been trying to say. I had lived with rage throughout my life – my mother's and father's rages against their poverty, their wants, the war, and all their losses. Not surprisingly, I took up this rage, as well as the troubled forms of love that spring out of that heat. As a woman I had been socialized against what are generally thought to be male attributes like pride, aggression, and disobedience to hierarchical authority. But I had been rarely called on the carpet to account for my sometimes unavoidable but oftentimes self-defeating survival tactics, such as submissiveness and manipulation and all the self-hatred, jealousies, and resentments that came with the rage.

For a working-class woman like me, pride was not my deadly sin. The danger for me had been self-denial – the ingrained sense of victimhood – that so often had allowed me to abdicate responsibility and let others act on my behalf. Rage is a spark, but it is not the fire, earth, water, or air of life. In the left and in the labour movement I have seen the self-defeating limitations of rage in social change. While it can be a worthy struggle, sometimes, to tap into collective rage, that element cannot be sustained, and it can't be used to build new power relations.

As I understand it, movements are about change. That's why, for example, we call the collective, forward-thinking activities of unions "the labour movement" and not "union station." But by the time people form themselves into a political party they have, by definition, created an institution concerned with policy, consensus, and recruiting members, and bringing in enough money to keep the creature alive. Parties need to win support for their platforms, and turn that support into votes. But electoral power does not necessarily mean change, as we have found out. Change has to start before it reaches a legislature. A legislature can enshrine change, it can promote change, but it can't start it. People make change.

And, I think, despite all the setbacks, we have been making change over the past two or three decades. We have learned, we have continued to strive for what we think might be a better way of doing things in this world. In *Long Way From Home: The Story of the Sixties Generation in Canada*, Myrna Kostash speculates that there are thousands of people in Canada who have not forgotten how they grew up and what they learned in redesigning a world, who continue to refine and apply their learning in everyday work and family lives, in their emotional, political, and cultural lives. There is no law either, she says, that says the times will never again erupt into revolt, or that there will never again be a generation of hot-heads. Among the new hotheads, perhaps, are late-bloomers like myself, people who once may have had little voice or power but who still worked hard in whatever tidy and untidy ways we could – who, along with our children, are still organizing, still caring, still struggling (and suffering).

Smashing capitalism, like smashing monogamy, was never as easy as it might have once seemed to me. That is why organizing for equity, food, jobs, shelter, education, health, culture, social services, social heritage, peace, and the environment are still on my political agenda, and probably always will be. I'm glad many other people still care about these issues. I'm glad there is a women's movement. I'm glad there is a labour movement to shove important issues onto the agendas of the political parties and government. But the next step, I believe, is the step towards a cultural revolution, fuelled by the spirits and energies of all our forces. There is not one leader, there are many leaders, among us. Each of us should be proud of whom we are and where we come from. To get to that revolution we must realize there are many roads to truth – there are many truths – and despite all the confusion of those many directions, each one of us, in shaping our own stories, is licensed to drive.